JOSEPH
HAYDN

CLASSIC *f*M LIFELINES

JOSEPH HAYDN

AN ESSENTIAL GUIDE TO HIS LIFE AND WORKS

NEIL WENBORN

PAVILION

First published in Great Britain in 1997 by
PAVILION BOOKS LIMITED
26 Upper Ground, London SE1 9PD

Copyright © Pavilion Books Ltd 1997
Front cover illustration © The Lebrecht Collection

Edited and designed by Castle House Press, Penarth, South Wales
Cover designed by Bet Ayer

A CIP catalogue record for this book is available
from the British Library

ISBN 1 86205 011 2

Set in Lydian and Caslon
Printed and bound in Great Britain by Mackays of Chatham

2 4 6 8 10 9 7 5 3 1

This book can be ordered direct from the publisher.
Please contact the Marketing Department.
But try your bookshop first.

Contents

ACKNOWLEDGMENTS

To Sue and Henry,
with love and gratitude

A NOTE FROM THE EDITORS

A biography of this type inevitably contains numerous references to pieces of music. The paragraphs are also peppered with 'quotation marks', since much of the tale is told through reported speech.

Because of this, and to make things more accessible for the reader as well as easier on the eye, we decided to simplify the method of typesetting the names of musical works. Conventionally this is determined by the nature of the individual work, following a set of rules whereby some pieces appear in italics, some in italics and quotation marks, others in plain roman type and others still in roman and quotation marks.

In this book, the names of all musical works are simply set in italics. Songs and arias appear in italics and quotation marks.

CHAPTER I

THE EARLY YEARS
(1732–49)

- ◆ Rohrau
- ◆ Hainburg
- ◆ The choirboy

Joseph Haydn stands alone in the history of music. Probably no other composer has contributed so much to so broad a variety of forms or been so widely loved and venerated in his own lifetime. His sheer fecundity is staggering – in the course of half a century he wrote some 107 symphonies, 68 string quartets, 62 piano sonatas, 45 piano trios, 14 masses, 24 operas, and the oratorios *The Creation* and *The Seasons*, to name only the most prominent forms represented in his phenomenal output. His long career, central to the establishment of the Viennese classical style, spans the late Baroque and the early Romantic periods. When he was born, Bach was still writing cantatas as cantor of St Thomas' in Leipzig; when he died, Beethoven had just published his *Pastoral Symphony*. More than any other single figure, it is Haydn, with his restless originality and seemingly inexhaustible richness of invention, who provides the bridge between the two eras.

Equally unparalleled is the posthumous fate of Haydn's work. At the end of the eighteenth century his position on the European musical stage was compared with that of Shakespeare in literature. By the end of the nineteenth, however, eclipsed by the towering reputations of Mozart, his devoted friend, and Beethoven, his wayward former pupil, his music had fallen spectacularly from grace; and only in the second half of the twentieth century, not least through the tireless advocacy of the great Haydn scholar H.C. Robbins Landon, has it come to re-establish its rightful place at the forefront of the classical canon.

Despite his international fame as a composer and the copious honours that flowed from it, it took some time for Haydn's two earliest biographers, Georg August Griesinger and Albert Christoph Dies, to persuade him that his life was worth writing about at all. For Haydn himself, by then the grand old man of the musical world, his life story could, he said, be summed up in the three words '*Vixi, scripsi, dixi* ' – 'I lived, I wrote, I spoke.'

But Haydn was famous for his modesty. If the outward circumstances of his life must often have seemed uneventful, his story is nonetheless by any standards a remarkable one – that of the peasant's son who, in an age of rigid social hierarchies that would have been quite familiar to his medieval ancestors, rose to become one of the world's greatest musicians, the toast of kings and perhaps the most celebrated living composer of all time.

ROHRAU

That story began in the village of Rohrau in Lower Austria on the afternoon of 31 March 1732. (Haydn himself always refuted the alternative date of 1 April for the same reasons that make it in some ways a more attractive one: there was undoubtedly a pronounced strain of practical joking in his make-up.) Franz Joseph Haydn – he was never to use his first baptismal name – was the second child of the village wheelwright, Mathias Haydn, and his wife, Anna Maria Koller, who had been a junior cook at the castle of the local landowner, Count Harrach.

The village of Rohrau, which lies in marshy countryside in the valley of the Leitha a few miles from the Hungarian border, had seen its share of physical changes in the preceding years. Subject to sometimes disastrous floods, it had also twice been razed to the ground during the Turkish Wars in which Haydn's own great-grandfather had been killed and which had brought the armies of the Ottoman Empire to the very gates of Vienna. Rohrau's social fabric, on the other hand, had barely changed since the Middle Ages. The local powers of the Harrach family were all but absolute and the gulf dividing their opulent lifestyle from the hard and uncertain lot of the peasantry seemingly unbridgeable.

There was nothing in the Haydn family background to presage Joseph's remarkable talent. Reminiscing to Dies and Griesinger in his old age, Haydn recalled how his father had learnt the harp in his travels as a journeyman and used to regale the fast-growing family with his songs, encouraging his wife and children to join in. This, however, was the extent of the musical life of a household that was to produce not only one of the greatest of classical composers but also two other professional musicians. Joseph's brother Michael (1737–1806), himself a composer of standing, would be employed in the archiepiscopal court in Salzburg, where he became a friend of the Mozarts, while his only other surviving brother Johann Evangelist (1743–1805) later worked under Haydn in the choir of his principal employers, the Esterházy family. Of the twelve children born to Mathias and Anna Maria, three sisters also survived to adulthood.

Even in his years of spectacular success, it was with these people and their class that Haydn's loyalties remained. As he was to say in later life, 'I have associated with emperors, kings, and many great gentlemen and have heard many flattering things from them; but I do not wish to live on an intimate footing with such persons, and I prefer people of my own status.' It was a loyalty that found expression not only in his lifelong support of family and friends but also in his music: many of his works contain echoes of the kind of folksongs he learned round the family hearth in Rohrau, and the stamping of peasant dancers can be heard in his minuets as frequently as the gracious strains of the society ballroom.

The Haydn household appears to have been a happy, industrious and above all a very orderly one. Joseph attributed his lifelong habits of cleanliness, neatness and sheer hard work to his mother's admonitions, and in his dealings with publishers he was to show the same acumen that helped his father attain the responsible local position of *Marktrichter* (literally 'market judge').

The Haydns were also a very religious family, and Joseph was to remain a devout Catholic throughout his life. (His surviving autograph scores typically begin with the words *In nomine Domini* and end with *Laus Deo*.) Indeed, his parents seem to have intended him for the priesthood, and Haydn himself believed that it was this, rather than any thought of a career in music, that determined them to further his musical education. Whatever their reasons, in 1738 little Sepperl, as they called him, was sent to the nearby town of Hainburg, where his father had been born and where his grandmother still lived, to study with one Johann Mathias Franck, a schoolteacher and choirmaster at the local church. It was perhaps the most decisive moment in his young life and one that was to change the course of musical history.

HAINBURG

By Haydn's own account, it had come about when Franck, a distant family connection, had visited the Haydns' cottage at Rohrau and had sat in on one of their musical evenings. He had noted Sepperl's unusually pure voice, which had already attracted admiration in the village, and the innate musical sense that led him to saw at his arm with a stick as if he were playing an accompaniment on the violin. Recognizing promise when he saw it, he suggested that he take charge of the boy's education, and the proud parents decided to accept the proposal. The departure for Hainburg was quickly arranged, and at the age of five Haydn left his birthplace for good, returning to Rohrau only for occasional visits thereafter.

For the next two years Franck was to cultivate Sepperl's musical gifts with all the rigour characteristic of an eighteenth-century Austrian education. In addition to the three Rs, Joseph was given a grounding in practical musicianship, singing in the choir and learning the rudiments of a wide range of instruments (including the drum, which the small boy was apparently enabled to play in one procession by having it strapped to the back of a hunchback walking in front of him!). He seems to have mastered the basics of the clavier and the violin, and may also have learnt to copy music from Franck's large collection of manuscripts.

Despite the harshness of the regimen and the uncongenial slovenliness of the Francks' household, in which he lived on equal terms with his teacher's children, Haydn remained grateful to Franck for the rest of his life for the all-round education of his Hainburg years. 'I shall owe it to this man even in my grave,' he told Griesinger more than fifty years later, 'that he set me to so many different things, although I received in the process more thrashings than food.' A portrait of his former teacher still hung in his house when he died, and with characteristic generosity he remembered Franck's daughter in his will.

In 1740, however, Haydn's life was to undergo another radical change, as once again his superior talents were recognized by a visiting musician. The visitor this time was Karl Georg Reutter, who had recently been appointed *Kapellmeister* (literally 'chapel master', effectively music director) of St Stephen's cathedral in Vienna and was scouting in Hainburg for new conscripts to the ranks of his choir. The priest with whom he was staying drew his attention to Joseph, and Reutter proceeded to put the boy through his musical paces. Haydn later recounted how, when Reutter asked him if he could sing a trill, he replied that not even Cousin Franck could do that (no doubt to the discomfiture of his teacher, who was in the room at the time). After a little instruction and a couple of false starts, however, Joseph mastered the art, and remembered being rewarded from a large bowl of cherries that stood on the priest's table.

A more significant prize was the offer of a place in the cathedral choir once he had reached the age of eight. Mathias and Anna Maria jumped at this new opportunity and quickly gave permission for their son to move to Vienna. Sepperl spent the intervening period teaching himself to sing scales in preparation for his new position – another indication, if Franck's inability to trill were not enough, that he had already passed the limit of his tutor's pedagogic skills. It was clearly time to move on.

THE CHOIRBOY

So it was that in April or May 1740 the eight-year-old Haydn arrived in the city that was to be his home for the next two decades, the scene, many years later, of some of his greatest triumphs, and a musical centre of gravity for him for the rest of his life.

Vienna in 1740 was the hub of the Habsburg domains, and the seat of both the court and the central administration of the Empire. The twenty-three-year-old Maria Theresa, who had just been crowned Queen of Hungary and Bohemia, was a familiar figure to the inhabitants of the city, and took a lively and, as Joseph was to discover to his cost, sometimes critical interest in its cultural life. Above all, Vienna was a Catholic city, its rhythms that of the church calendar to which the routines of the choir were inextricably linked.

The focus of those routines, which left little leisure for the six choirboys or their older colleagues, was St Stephen's itself. The great Gothic cathedral, with its soaring 400-foot spire, was the physical and spiritual centre of Vienna and, then as now, the city's dominant landmark. Haydn, who lived next door in the choir school, was required to sing two services in the cathedral every day, and if to the more cosmopolitan eyes of the musicologist Charles Burney it was later to appear 'dark, dirty, and dismal', its ranks of dusty trophies and rotting flags making it look like 'an old warehouse', it must nonetheless have been an awe-inspiring sight to young Sepperl after the provincial churches of Rohrau and Hainburg.

In addition to these fixed appointments, the choir sang at numerous religious, court and civic functions, such as feast days, processions and funerals (probably including that of Antonio Vivaldi, who died in poverty in Vienna in 1741). They also made themselves available for 'academies', or private concerts at the houses of the Viennese nobility, and Joseph seems quickly to have spotted the well-stocked tables at these events as a useful means of supplementing his meagre diet at the choir school, which he later described as 'a continual fast'.

It was not only Sepperl's stomach that suffered from the privations of the austere regime at the choir school. His general education too seems to have been neglected. Despite Burney's later dismissal of Georg Reutter's numerous compositions as exhibiting 'great noise and little meaning', the *Kapellmeister* was an experienced and extremely popular composer who was already well on his way to acquiring a near-monopoly of the city's key musical posts. This accumulation of jobs led to a busy life, in which the demands of St Stephen's, and in particular the education of the choristers, seem to have been early casualties. Reminiscing to Griesinger in his old age, Haydn recalled only 'the scant instruction usual at the time, in Latin, in religion, in arithmetic and writing'.

His musical education seems to have been little better. Dies, also drawing on conversations with the composer, claimed Joseph was taught no more than was required for him to fulfil his duties as a chorister. Griesinger gives a fuller picture, but one that redounds only marginally more to Reutter's credit:

> . . . *Haydn had in the Choir School very capable instructors on several instruments, and especially in singing. Among the latter were Gegenbauer, a functionary of the Court Chorus, and an*

elegant tenor, Finsterbusch. No instruction in music theory was undertaken in the Choir School, and Haydn remembered receiving only two lessons in this from the excellent Reutter. But Reutter did encourage him to make whatever variations he liked on the motets and Salves *that he had to sing through in the church, and this practice early led him to ideas of his own which Reutter corrected.*

If direct tuition was limited, however, the opportunities for self-instruction were enormous, especially for someone as determined and single-minded as the young Haydn. The musical life of Vienna was in transition, after the recent deaths not only of the music-loving Emperor Charles VI, but also of the musical luminaries of his court, the composers Johann Joseph Fux and Antonio Caldara, both masters of the late Baroque. Their music, though, could still be heard throughout the capital, and Haydn undoubtedly benefited from exposure to it and the work of lesser contemporaries. Later he was to say 'I listened more than I studied, but I heard the finest music in all forms that was to be heard in my time, and of this there was much in Vienna. . . . I listened attentively and tried to turn to good account what most impressed me. Thus little by little my knowledge and my ability were developed.'

To this period, too, seems to belong his acquisition of two classic works of musical theory, Mattheson's *Der vollkommene Kapellmeister* (published in 1739) and Fux's *Gradus ad Parnassum* (1725), a well-thumbed copy of which he still retained in old age. He worked his way through Fux's contrapuntal exercises with unstinting application (and was later to use them in teaching his own students, including Beethoven). As characteristic as his diligence, however, is his self-deprecating account of his attempts to apply what he had learned to composition in eight and sixteen parts: 'I used to think then that it was all right if only the paper were pretty full,' he told Griesinger. 'Reutter laughed at my immature output, at measures no throat and no instrument could have executed, and he scolded me for composing for sixteen parts before I even understood two-part setting.' Dies tells a similar story of Reutter finding the boy engaged in writing a twelve-part *Salve Regina* and deriding him with 'Aren't two voices enough for you, you little blockhead?'

These, then, were Haydn's first stumbling attempts at composition. But life as a choirboy in Vienna was not all study and hardship. There were lighter moments too, in which Joseph's youthful high spirits can be glimpsed across the centuries. For example, he recalled being the ringleader when the choristers visited the newly-completed Schönbrunn palace on the outskirts of the city and clambered all over the scaffolding, which had not yet been taken down. As they were doing so, the Empress herself appeared, disturbed by the racket, and ordered one of her staff to chase them away, threatening any who returned with a good hiding. Undaunted, Sepperl climbed again the following day and was duly thrashed.

Joseph's mischievous streak was shared by his brother Michael, who followed him into the choir in 1745 at the age of eight. Pleased as Joseph must initially have been to have his brother's company, however, it soon became apparent that Michael also stood fair to succeed him as the cathedral's star soprano. Indeed, the younger boy was more precocious than Joseph, both musically and intellectually, and anyone meeting the brothers at this time would have thought him the one more likely to be destined for a glittering musical career.

It was not just that Michael was the faster learner. Joseph's voice, his passport to both Hainburg and Vienna, was about to break – Maria Theresa herself had complained that 'Joseph Haydn doesn't sing any more; he crows.' Things were coming full circle. Reutter had travelled to Hainburg in 1740 looking for fresh talent to replace choristers whose voices were breaking. Now Joseph's own turn was rapidly approaching.

What happened next, if Haydn's later friends are to be believed, has all the constituents of black farce. It seems that Reutter suggested castration to Joseph as a means of preserving his voice. An appeal to Mathias for permission brought the wheelwright post-haste from Rohrau. Griesinger's second-hand account of the ensuing meeting has Mathias, thinking the operation might already have been performed, entering the room with the tentative words 'Sepperl, does anything hurt you? Can you still walk?' Finding he wasn't too late, he put paid to the scheme once and for all, a decision in which he was apparently strongly supported by a *castrato* who happened to be present. It all sounds too theatrical to be true, and even if Haydn did retail the story to friends and pupils in old age, one should perhaps not forget that he was no less given to embroidering the facts than most people who know a good anecdote when they see one.

Whatever the truth of the matter, Joseph's days at St Stephen's were clearly numbered. For reasons we shall never know, Reutter made no attempt to keep him on in another capacity, and seems to have leapt at the first opportunity that presented itself to dismiss him. Typically enough, the occasion was provided by one of Joseph's practical jokes. He mischievously cut off the pigtail of one of the other choristers. It was a prank too many, and Reutter sentenced him to a caning on the palm of his hand. Haydn, by now seventeen, felt such a punishment was below his dignity and declared that he would rather leave the choir school forthwith than submit to it. Reutter is said to have replied: 'That won't work! . . . First you'll be caned, and then get out!' and was as good as his word.

It was November 1749. Haydn had been in Vienna for a little over nine years. Apart from his musical training, all he had to show for it were the three shirts and threadbare coat with which he left the choir school. With no money in his pocket, nowhere to live and no prospect of employment, the capital must have presented a very different aspect from the city of promise he had entered as a child in 1740.

The next few years were to be the most difficult of his life.

CHAPTER 2
FREELANCE IN VIENNA
(1750–61)

- ♦ *'Utmost poverty'*
- ♦ A *growing reputation*
- ♦ *Kapellmeister to Count Morzin*

Haydn's decade as a jobbing musician remains a period of biographical shadow, through which it is often difficult even to discern the order of known events. Of his everyday activities we catch only fleeting glimpses, refracted through the anecdotes he told in his old age and such scanty documentary evidence as has survived from these crucial years in his development as a composer. What is not in doubt is the hardness of his life during most of this time. It was to this period that Haydn was referring when he told Dies that 'what I am today is the product of utmost poverty'.

As Mozart was to discover some forty years later, the life of a self-employed musician in eighteenth-century Vienna was at best a precarious one. When Mozart launched himself into freelance life, however, the afterglow of his phenomenal childhood successes still clung to him. He was already well-known as a composer and well-connected among the Viennese nobility. Above all, he could lay claim to being the greatest keyboard virtuoso of his time. The seventeen-year-old Haydn, on the other hand, was entirely unknown, a mere apprentice in the art of composition, and unskilled at any particular instrument. The future for him looked bleak indeed.

'UTMOST POVERTY'

So, at least in the short term, it was to prove. Left homeless on his abrupt departure from the choir school, his most pressing need was for somewhere to live. In the first of a series of near-providential encounters that strewed his path in these years, he almost immediately bumped into one Johann Michael Spangler, a fellow-singer. With a generosity beyond the call of duty, Spangler offered to put Haydn up in his cramped garret, despite the fact that he was already sharing it with a wife and a nine-month-old baby son.

To solve the problem of accommodation, albeit temporarily, was one thing. Making a living was quite a different matter. Haydn's parents, no doubt horrified at the turn of events and unable to support him financially, seem to have revived their ambition for him to become a priest, but Joseph stood firm against their persuasion. There seems to have been a time shortly after his dismissal, however, when he considered entering the Servite Order simply in order to be able to eat.

In the autobiographical sketch he provided for an Austrian cultural magazine in 1776, he wrote of this time that he 'had to eke out a wretched existence for eight whole years, by teaching young pupils'. But giving lessons at the miserable rate of two gulden a month was no way to live, and during this period we see him making determined efforts to find additional sources of income by promoting himself within the musical establishment, picking up contacts, temporary appointments and, consequently, fees along the way.

In the spring of 1750, for example, he went on pilgrimage to the famous shrine at Mariazell in the Styrian Alps, taking with him some motets of his own composition. While there, he tried to persuade the choirmaster, who was himself an alumnus of the St Stephen's choir school, to take him on as a singer now that his voice had settled, but he was turned down flat. With a persistence no doubt born of desperation, Haydn insinuated himself into the choir the following day, snatched the music from another chorister and sang from it so well that the choirmaster invited him to stay for a week – during which time he made good the food deficit of months.

At about this time a new addition to Spangler's family (a baby girl whom we shall meet again as a soprano at the Esterházy court) forced Haydn to move into new lodgings. It was another garret, up under the eaves of the Old Michaelerhaus, next door to St

Michael's church where Spangler sang; but this time he was on his own. Despite the wretched conditions – the roof leaked and there was no heating or natural light – Haydn seems to have relished the independence: 'when I was sitting at my old worm-eaten clavier,' he told Griesinger, 'I envied no king his lot.' His circumstances were made a little more comfortable, too, by the financial assistance of a local tradesman, Anton Buchholz. Haydn, whose memory for such acts of kindness was of a piece with his own generosity of spirit, included in his will of 1801 a touching legacy of a hundred florins to 'Fräulein Anna Buchholz . . . inasmuch as in my youth her grandfather lent me one hundred and fifty florins when I greatly needed them, which, however, I repaid fifty years ago.'

The repayment of the loan shows in itself that there was money coming in, albeit from disparate and casual sources. In addition to his teaching commitments, Haydn had apparently secured the post of first violinist at the Convent of the Hospitallers in the Leopoldstadt, for which he was paid a small annual stipend. In return he had to play in church on Sunday mornings at eight o'clock. From there he went straight to the chapel of Count Haugwitz, where he played the organ at ten o'clock (and for which he probably wrote most of his early organ concertos), then to St Stephen's to sing, now as a tenor, at 11.00a.m. He also played in the bands of touring serenaders who were such a characteristic feature of the Viennese summer evenings and whose music, especially in its use of the wind band (*Harmonie-musik*) was to leave an enduring mark on the textures of his own compositions.

A number of his earliest works were written for such groups, including probably the *Quintet in G* (II:2). (Haydn's works are most consistently designated by the groups and numbers within groups given them by the scholar Anthony van Hoboken; thus II:2 indicates the second work of the second group, 'Divertimenti (without keyboard) in four parts and over'.)

His serenading activities also involved him in two other encounters of note. The first, which shows his mischievous spirits undaunted by adversity, was a close brush with the police when he gathered a group of fellow-serenaders in the insalubrious *Tiefer Graben* and issued each of them with different music. Local residents called out the contemporary equivalent of the riot squad to put paid to the resulting cacophony.

The second encounter was far more auspicious. One evening in 1751 or 1752, Haydn and his band were playing one of his serenades under the windows of the handsome wife of a celebrated comic actor, 'Bernardon' Kurz, when Kurz himself appeared and asked who the composer was. Haydn came forward and Kurz urged him to write the music for a satirical opera he was planning. The result, *Der krumme Teufel* (The crooked devil), was performed at the prestigious Kärntnerthortheater in May 1753 and was a marked success at the box office. Despite being taken off after three nights when the presumed object of its satire registered a complaint, it remained in the repertoire well into the 1770s, but the music, for which Haydn was paid a modest one-off fee, has not survived. That he retained happy memories of its composition is evident in the affectionate anecdotes he told his biographers of Kurz's eccentric behaviour.

His choice of lodging proved equally fortuitous. If his fellow tenants under the eaves were labourers and petty artisans, the Old Michaelerhaus was also home to some of the most exalted figures in Austrian cultural life. On the first floor lived the Dowager Princess Maria Octavia Esterházy, in the service of whose two sons, Paul Anton and Nicolaus, Haydn would spend the majority of his career. Of more immediate importance to him, though, were the occupants of the third floor, which housed the apartments of the Imperial Court Poet Pietro Metastasio.

Metastasio, a prolific librettist whose work was set more than 800 times by operatic composers, shared these apartments with a Spanish family called Martinez whose two daughters he was helping to educate. The eldest child, Marianne, was already exhibiting the talents that would establish her as something of a Viennese bluestocking. (She was later to be a great favourite of Mozart, who played piano duets with her.) How Haydn's path crossed Metastasio's in this socially stratified house we do not know, but the great man took the struggling young musician on as Marianne's piano teacher in exchange for free board. The arrangement continued for three years, during which time Haydn made an even more important contact in Marianne's singing teacher, the Neapolitan composer Nicola Porpora.

Once a leading figure in the musical world, Porpora, who had tried unsuccessfully to set up in England as a rival to Handel in the 1730s, was by now an embittered old man, but his musical knowledge and undoubted skills as a teacher were to be of tremendous value to Haydn. The young man offered his services as an accompanist and became in effect Porpora's musical valet – by no means an unusual combination of roles in the eighteenth century and one which had set Mozart's father Leopold on the first step of his own musical career only a few years earlier. Haydn's account of their relationship is colourful and succinct: 'There was no lack of *Asino*, *Coglione*, *Birbante* [ass, jerk, rascal], and pokes in the ribs, but I put up with it all, for I profited greatly with Porpora in singing, in composition, and in the Italian language.'

It had been the running frustration of Haydn's musical life to date that he had had no proper teachers of theory and that his efforts to make ends meet left little time for study unless, as he often did, he worked into the early hours of the morning. That was now changing. Not only was Porpora giving him the benefit of his experience; he had also come across the recently published keyboard sonatas of Carl Philipp Emanuel Bach, son of the great but at this time largely forgotten Johann Sebastian, and they acted on him with the force of revelation. 'Whoever knows me thoroughly,' he told Griesinger, 'must discover that I owe a great deal to Emanuel Bach, that I understood him and have studied him diligently. Emanuel Bach once made me a compliment on this score himself.'

Porpora also provided Haydn with his first access to the nobility. He was singing teacher to the mistress of the Venetian ambassador and took Haydn with him when he accompanied her on visits to the ambassador's summer residence in the fashionable spa town of Mannersdorf. Here the young man seems to have attended the celebrated academies of the Prince of Hildburghausen and met some of the leading composers of the day, including the operatic genius Christoph Willibald Gluck and the symphonist Georg Christoph Wagenseil.

He may also have taken the opportunity to visit Rohrau, which was within easy striking distance of Mannersdorf. We know that both Joseph and Michael returned to the family cottage from time to time and that the musical evenings continued, though the greater sophistication of the two brothers seems to have led to some minor domestic disharmony on these occasions. More radical changes also occurred within the family circle at about this time, with the death of Haydn's mother in 1754 at the age of 47 and Mathias' remarriage to a servant girl three years Joseph's junior. In 1754, too, Michael left Vienna for Hungary, where in 1757 he took up the post of *Kapellmeister* to the Bishop of Gross-wardein (now in Romania). He was only twenty. His twenty-five-year-old brother would have to wait another two years before securing his own first real appointment.

A GROWING REPUTATION

By the second half of the 1750s, however, Haydn's star was clearly rising. In 1758 he revised *Der krumme Teufel*, presumably for a revival. Furthermore, manuscript copies of his instrumental and chamber music already seem to have been selling briskly through Viennese booksellers (albeit at no profit to the composer), and led to his being sought out by at least one influential patroness, Countess Thun, to whom he gave lessons.

Another illustrious contact was Carl Joseph von Fürnberg, at whose country seat, Weinzierl Castle, near Melk in Lower Austria, Haydn was an occasional guest. And it is with one such visit that the origins of the string quartet are indelibly associated.

Of the two forms Haydn is popularly credited with originating, the symphony and the string quartet, only the latter can truly be claimed as his own invention. The perfectly balanced combination of two violins, viola and cello – often regarded as the purest of all musical mediums – was early recognized as a central and distinctive achievement of the Viennese classical school, and there was much speculation during Haydn's own lifetime as to where he got the idea from. Griesinger asked him about it during their conversations and there appears no reason to doubt Haydn's reply that it was a pure accident.

According to his account, the Baron von Fürnberg invited Haydn, the local priest, his estate manager and Albrechtsberger (almost certainly the same one who later taught Beethoven) for musical gatherings at Weinzierl and not unnaturally asked Haydn to write something for the combination of instruments they played. It is thus to a chance combination of instrumentalists at an aristocratic musical party, probably around 1757, that we owe not only the majority of the quartets later collected for publication as Haydn's Opp.1 & 2, but also one of his most important and most wholly characteristic contributions to the development of Western music.

Slight as these early five-movement quartets are, compared with his later great works in the form, they were immediately recognized as the product of an original musical mind, and were to prove highly influential (though Haydn himself, who like most eighteenth-century composers wrote almost exclusively to commission for specific occasions, did not return to the string quartet for another decade). For example, we find Haydn performing them at Harrach Castle in the late 1750s (and what a sign of the growing strength of his reputation that the Rohrau overlord should now have the wheelwright's son as his guest). A Prussian prisoner of war who was billeted there at the time described the composer as 'modest to the point of timidity, despite the fact that everybody present was enchanted by these compositions'.

With hindsight, there are signs of what was to come even in the first quartet of all (Op.1 No.1), where the trio of the second minuet, with its G minor canon between two violins, foreshadows almost uncannily the famous 'witches' minuet' of Op.76 No.2 (1796) and already shows Haydn using counterpoint to add sinew to his instrumental writing. There are scattered pieces for four solo strings among the works of Haydn's older contemporaries, but it is these quartets – Haydn still calls them *divertimenti a quattro* – that stand at the beginning of the string quartet tradition.

Haydn seems to have written prolifically in other forms too during his years as a freelance, but much of this music has disappeared and it is impossible to date most of what may remain with any confidence. We know he wrote various sacred vocal works, such as the motets he took to Mariazell in 1750; and if Haydn's memory did not fail him, the *Missa brevis in F* (XXII:1), which he rediscovered in old age, may be his earliest surviving composition (1749). A number of his simpler keyboard sonatas and string trios probably also belong to this first Viennese period, the former almost certainly written for the use of his various pupils; and some early divertimenti for strings and wind are no doubt the legacy of his serenading activities. His only dated instrumental composition from this time, however, is the *Organ Concerto in C* (XVIII:1) of 1756, the occasion of which, and of the *Salve Regina* in E (XXIIIb:1) (also 1756), we shall have cause to mention later.

KAPELLMEISTER TO COUNT MORZIN

It was probably through Fürnberg that Haydn met the man who gave him his first real appointment, Ferdinand Maximilian Franz, Count Morzin. The precise date of this important event, as of so much else in this period, is uncertain, but it was probably in 1759 that Haydn became *Kapellmeister* to Count Morzin at a salary of 200 gulden a year, with free board and lodging. The count divided his time between Vienna and his country castle at Lukaveč, near Pilsen in Bohemia, where he spent the summer months, and it seems reasonable to assume that his new music director did likewise. Morzin kept a small string orchestra, which was joined from time to time by members of his wind band, and Haydn wrote music for both, including divertimenti for social occasions such as suppers, hunting parties and picnics.

It is with the Morzin orchestra that the most important of his early compositions – the first symphonies – are associated, though it is possible that some were actually written just before he joined the count's household. As has already been mentioned, Haydn used once to be regarded as the 'father of the symphony', and his was certainly the most important voice in shaping the form that was to become a cornerstone of the classical repertoire from the eighteenth to the twentieth century. However, he was by no means its inventor. If anything, he came relatively late to a tradition already represented, among others, by such eminent composers as Johann Stamitz in Mannheim and the imperial court composer Wagenseil in Vienna.

It would be wrong, too, to invest the symphony of the 1750s with the totemic significance it would have a century later. The borders of the form were still porous, and the terms symphony, overture, partita and divertimento still largely interchangeable. (For example, the fifth of the string quartets published as Op.1 is really a symphony.) Haydn's earliest contributions to the form are the equal of his contemporaries', but they remain slight in comparison with his symphonies of ten years later, let alone the great '*London*' *Symphonies* of the 1790s.

The precise chronology of Haydn's 107 extant symphonies remains a matter of conjecture. The numbers given them by the eminent Austrian scholar Eusebius von Mandyczewski in 1907 and preserved by Hoboken, and by which they are still generally known, bear only a broad resemblance to the order in which they were written (to give the most extreme example, No.72 was probably composed at about the same time as Nos.13 & 31). Comfortingly, though, Haydn's first symphony does seem to be the one known as No.1. The other symphonies that belong to the Morzin years, or at least to the period before Haydn joined the Esterházy household in May 1761, are Nos.2–5, 10, 11, 15, 18, 27, 32, 33 and 37, as well as the symphony known as 'A'; 19, 20, 25 and 'B' may also have been written at this time. The works employ a variety of forms: some, such as No.1, are in three movements (fast-slow-fast); others in four; and some, such as Nos.5, 11 and 18, have opening slow movements in the *sonata da chiesa* tradition. Haydn's lifelong tendency to develop movements from motivic seeds rather than from fully-fledged melodies is already evident, as is his integration of contrapuntal and homophonic textures, most conspicuously perhaps in No.3. Equally apparent is his leaning towards irregular phrase-lengths, as in the six-bar theme of the last movement of the *First Symphony*, and his use of the wind band is already distinctive.

Little is known about this period as *Kapellmeister* to Count Morzin, though according to Griesinger, Haydn 'used to like to tell in his later years how, when he was sitting once at the clavier and the beautiful Countess Morzin was bending over him to see the notes, her neckerchief came undone. "It was the first time I had seen such a sight," he recalled; "it embarrassed me, my playing faltered, my fingers stopped on the keys." ' It is perhaps not fanciful to connect the susceptibility revealed in this vignette with the fact that in November 1760 he married Maria Anna Keller, the eldest daughter of a wigmaker who had been helpful to him in his early career (and who seems to have urged the union with some determination). Haydn had in fact been in love with Maria Anna's sister, Therese, but she had entered a convent in 1756 – her vows being the occasion for which he had written the organ concerto and *Salve Regina* mentioned earlier. Unlike Mozart's marriage under strangely similar circumstances, Haydn's relationship with his first love's sister quickly deteriorated. According to his own account, which is of course the only side of the story we have, Maria Anna was domineering, irresponsible and profligate with his income. Perhaps more damaging still, she appears, despite having once been his pupil, to have had no musical sense: 'it is all the same to her,' he was later to say, 'if her husband is a shoemaker or an artist.' Loveless and childless, the marriage lasted, in name at least, until Maria Anna's death in 1800, though Haydn was quite open about his infidelities: 'My wife was unable to bear children,' was his laconic summary, 'and I was therefore less indifferent to the charms of other ladies.'

Haydn was in fact forbidden to marry under the terms of his contract of employment with Morzin, but this was not the reason for his leaving the count's service shortly afterwards. Morzin ran into financial difficulties, and within a couple of years of Haydn's appointment had to disband his orchestra as a cost-cutting exercise. By then, however, the brilliant young *Kapellmeister* had already caught the attention of Prince Paul Anton Esterházy, and on 1 May 1761 the prince officially appointed him Vice-*Kapellmeister* to his household. Haydn was to remain in the service of the family for the rest of his life.

CHAPTER 3

IN THE SERVICE OF THE ESTERHAZYS
(1761–66)

- ♦ The Esterházys
- ♦ Eisenstadt
- ♦ House officer to Prince Nicolaus

The Esterházys were one of the greatest of all central European noble houses. As Hungary's leading family, their fortunes had been made supporting the Habsburgs' campaign for the Hungarian crown, and were inextricably bound to those of the ruling dynasty. Created hereditary Princes of the Holy Roman Empire by a grateful emperor, they now commanded staggering wealth and influence, and their estates covered hundreds of thousands of acres in Austria, Hungary and beyond.

Prince Paul Anton, the head of the family, was 51, a distinguished former soldier and ambassador, and a man of broad cultural and intellectual interests. He played the violin, the flute and the lute, collected musical manuscripts, and maintained an orchestra and choir of such quality that Eisenstadt, his palace near Vienna, was already known as a centre of musical excellence. His aged *Kapellmeister*, Gregor Joseph Werner, was a distinguished composer, especially of church music, but he had occupied his post for more than thirty years and the demands of the job were now too much for him.

EISENSTADT

The palace at Eisenstadt was a fitting reflection of the Esterházys' social position. It was (and still is) a magnificent edifice, surrounded by elaborate formal gardens, with its own theatre and some 200 guest-rooms. Here the family, and therefore Haydn, spent their summers; in winter they stayed in Vienna.

Haydn's surviving contract of employment lays out the duties and responsibilities of the new Vice-*Kapellmeister* in exhaustive detail. The workload entailed is phenomenal. Although technically Werner's second-in-command, Haydn was effectively in sole charge of the prince's musical establishment. In addition to his duties as composer and conductor, he was therefore required to manage the administrative affairs of that establishment, which included looking after the music collection, the instruments, and what we would now call personnel matters – hiring and firing, training, employee relations, discipline, etc. He was enjoined to 'abstain from undue familiarity' with his musicians and 'from eating and drinking and other intercourse with them, so as to maintain the respect due to him'. He was also required to present himself twice daily in full livery to 'inquire whether his Highness is pleased to order a performance of the orchestra'. On receipt of the prince's orders he was to 'communicate them to the other musicians, and take care to be punctual at the appointed time, and to ensure punctuality in his subordinates, making a note of those who arrive late or absent themselves altogether.' Most important of all for his future career (and for posterity) was the fourth clause of the contract:

> *The said Vice-*Kapellmeister *shall be under obligation to compose such music as His Serene Highness may command, and neither to communicate such compositions to any other person, nor to allow them to be copied, but he shall retain them for the exclusive use of His Highness, and not compose for any other person without the knowledge and gracious permission of His Highness.*

Haydn's official salary was 400 gulden – the same as Werner's – but he was actually paid 600 (three times his Morzin wage), together with benefits in kind. It was explicitly understood that, all things being equal, he would succeed Werner as *Kapellmeister* in due course.

Demeaning as these terms may seem to the modern eye, they were altogether typical for the time. Indeed, the Esterházys were very much at the liberal end of the spectrum of noble employers; for example, they provided pensions and free medical care for their staff. There is no doubt that Haydn would have regarded himself as exceptionally well placed. He was, nonetheless, a servant, albeit a senior one (a 'house officer') at the beck and call of his lord, liable to summary dismissal or even imprisonment at his behest, and addressed in the third person even when he was present.

The orchestra he inherited was tiny by modern standards – no more than fifteen strong – but, as can be seen from the music he now began to compose for it, some of which remains taxing even for today's performers, it must have been a band of virtuosi. Haydn was to add to their number as time went on, notably by doubling the horns to four in 1763, a combination the possibilities of which he immediately explored in *Symphonies Nos.13, 31 (Horn-signal)* and *72*.

The calibre of the players also stimulated him to produce a cluster of concertos for them over the next few years. These include violin concertos for the leader, the famous virtuoso Luigi Tomasini (VIIa:1, 3 & 4); two cello concertos for Joseph Weigl (including VIIb:1, now one of Haydn's most popular works, although amazingly unrediscovered until 1961); harpsichord concertos, probably for himself to play; and flute and double-bass concertos which are now lost. The *Horn Concerto in D* (VIId:3), which also dates from these years, was probably composed for the Viennese virtuoso Joseph Leutgeb, for whom Mozart was later to write his own horn concertos. (Leutgeb seems to have been an amiable personality: Mozart's autographs are peppered with jokes at his expense, and Haydn scribbled 'written while asleep' on his.) After this burst of concerto-writing in the early 1760s, Haydn revisited the genre only sporadically and seems never to have been fully at home in it.

His first commission as Vice-*Kapellmeister*, though, was for a trilogy of symphonies representing the three times of day – morning, midday and evening – which are now known as Nos.6 (*Le matin*), 7 (*Le midi*) and 8 (*Le soir*). There is a freshness and verve to these works in which one can sense the composer feeling firm ground under his feet for the first time in his career. The earliest of Haydn's symphonies to find a regular place in the modern repertoire, they in fact look back to the Baroque *concerto grosso* for many of their characteristics. Concertante elements are well to the fore, giving most of the players in the band (including the double-bass player in the trios) plenty of opportunity to show off their solo skills – an early example of the diplomacy that was to form so large a part of Haydn's new job. They also incorporate some programmatic elements, though fewer than their titles might suggest. *Le matin* begins with a short evocation o~~f~~ and its second movement with a parody of the ki~~n~~ ing lessons Haydn gave himself in Hainburg. highly stylized thunderstorm, the flute prov as it would forty years later in the summer st great oratorio, *The Seasons*.

Hearing these showcase works in the gre palace, Prince Paul Anton must have congratu choice of music director. But he was not to e long. Already a sick man, the prince died in N succeeded by his brother, Prince Nicolaus, w serve for the next three decades.

HOUSE OFFICER TO PRINCE NICOLAUS

Nicolaus Esterházy was an even more passior Paul Anton. A complex and somewhat obses: was also a man who believed in living up to which led his contemporaries to dub him 'the the years, Haydn was to establish with him a w of mutual respect bordering as nearly on friendship as the gulf between their social stations permitted.

Among the first compositions Haydn produced for his new prince were two works for the stage: an Italian comic opera, *La Marchesa Nespola* (1762); and *Acide*, a *festa teatrale* for the prince's son's wedding in January 1763. Only parts of these works have survived, but they are an early earnest of the ever-increasing part opera would play in Haydn's life in the Esterházy household.

One genre that is hardly represented among the numerous compositions of Haydn's Eisenstadt years is church music, since under the terms of his contract of employment this remained the province of the nominal *Kapellmeister* Gregor Werner. Haydn seems to have gone out of his way to respect Werner's sensitivities, but relations between the two men nonetheless rapidly deteriorated. In October 1765 Werner wrote to Prince Nicolaus in the bitterest terms, denouncing his younger colleague for 'gross negligence' in his running of the musical establishment, and accusing him of allowing lax behaviour and chronic absenteeism among the musicians, failing to catalogue the music collection, letting the instruments go to rack and ruin, and lending out the church music indiscriminately.

Whatever the truth of these accusations, the prince responded with a stiff order to Haydn to run a tighter ship, and 'to hold in our absence two musical concerts every week in the Officers' room at Eisenstadt, *viz.*, on Tuesdays and Saturdays from 2 to 4 o'clock in the afternoon'. The final paragraph runs:

> *Finally, said* Capel Meister [sic] *Haydn is urgently enjoined to apply himself to composition more diligently than heretofore, and especially to write such pieces as can be played on the gamba, of which pieces we have seen very few up to now; and to be able to judge his diligence, he shall at all times send us the first copy, clearly and carefully written, of each and every new composition.*

Galling though it must have been to the already overworked composer, this order had two important effects. First, it led Haydn to begin a catalogue of all the works he could remember having written so far, presumably to prove the extent of his 'diligence'. This thematic catalogue, which he was to maintain with varying degrees of consistency up to the 1790s, is known as the *Entwurf-Katalog* (draft catalogue) and provides crucial evidence about his compositions.

Secondly, it opened the gate to a flood of works for the baryton (the 'gamba' of the prince's order). This instrument, already obsolescent, was a rather ungainly species of viola da gamba, with additional strings behind the neck which provided extra resonance and could also be plucked. It was something of an addiction with the prince, and over the next decade or so Haydn was to write some 160 works for him to play on it, including 126 trios for baryton, viola and cello, without which the instrument would now be of purely historical interest. In the end, Nicolaus' infatuation seems to have waned as rapidly as it grew, perhaps because Haydn, hoping to improve his compositions for it, ill-advisedly learned to play the instrument himself. There was, however, no repetition of the accusation of laziness, and by

January 1766 we find the prince sending Haydn a gift of 12 ducats in satisfaction at his latest pieces.

As in the earlier period, though, it is still Haydn's symphonies that embody his most consistently distinctive work. To the Eisenstadt years belong not only Nos.6–8 and the three four-horn symphonies mentioned above (Nos.13, 31 & 72), but also Nos.9, 12, 14, 16, 17, 21–24, 28–30, 36 & 40, bringing to about thirty the total of symphonies written between 1757–58 and 1763. Most of the Eisenstadt symphonies are in four movements with the minuet generally placed third, a pattern that was to become the norm for the classical symphony. Concertante elements are even more prominent now: the *adagio* of No.24, for example, gives an idea of what Haydn's lost flute concerto might have sounded like, while the finale of No.31 (*Hornsignal*) is a set of variations each of which (with one exception) features a different solo instrument or group – oboes, cello, flute, horns, violin and double bass – bringing the members of the Esterházy band vividly to life for us. Counterpoint continues to play a crucial part in Haydn's thinking: the finale of No.40, for example, is a fugue, while that of No.13 is based on the same four-note theme that Mozart would use in the towering last movement of his *Jupiter Symphony* more than twenty years later. No.22, nicknamed (obscurely) the *Philosopher*, features a chorale-like theme in its first movement, and No.30 (*Alleluja*) a Gregorian plainchant of the kind Haydn would use to devastating effect in his *Lamentatione Symphony* (No.26) a couple of years later.

The Eisenstadt years saw developments in Haydn's private life too. In 1763 his father, who had been touchingly proud to see his son established at last, died after a woodpile fell on him at work. The same year, his brother Michael moved to Salzburg as *Konzertmeister* to Archbishop Schrattenbach. (Also on the archbishop's payroll was the newly promoted deputy *Kapellmeister*, Leopold Mozart, who was about to set off on a grand European tour to promote the staggering talents of his seven-year-old son Wolfgang). In 1765 his other brother Johann Evangelist joined the Esterházy choir at Haydn's request (and expense). Then in March 1766 the long-ailing Werner died, and Haydn officially acceded to the post of *Kapellmeister*.

A far more significant change in the pattern of Haydn's life was about to take place, however. In the years before his accession to the princedom, Nicolaus had lived in a remote and (by Ester-házy standards) modest hunting-lodge on the family estates at Süttör in Hungary. He had become deeply attached to the place and had for some time been directing the erection of a vast palace there, to which he intended to relocate his court for part of the year. In 1766 this astonishing architectural project, though by no means completed, was deemed ready for habitation.

The prince called it Eszterháza, and it was to play a central part in the shaping of Haydn's musical development over the years to come.

CHAPTER 4

'THE LITTLE VERSAILLES IN HUNGARY'

(1766–76)

- ◆ *Isolation*
- ◆ *Sturm und Drang*
- ◆ *Life at Eszterháza*

Eszterháza was huge in conception as well as in scale. Dubbed 'the little Versailles in Hungary' by one of the many aristocratic visitors who flocked to see it over the years, it was a triumph of art over nature. The locality, on the south side of the Neusiedler See, was remote and swampy, and a major drainage operation had to be mounted before construction work could even begin. The whole enterprise soaked up astronomical sums of money, but no amount of expenditure could change the area's climate. Subject to scything winds in winter and mosquito infestation in summer, Eszterháza was a profoundly unhealthy place, and Haydn and his musicians were frequently ill during their sojourns there.

It was also undoubtedly one of the grandest noble palaces in Europe. Its attractions, lovingly detailed in the guidebook Prince Nicolaus caused to be written in the 1780s, included extensive formal gardens and hunting grounds, elaborate cascades, orangeries, a Chinese pavilion, classical temples, and a menagerie. The interior incorporated two great halls for entertainments, a suite of 126 guest rooms, a library of some 8,000 volumes, and a magnificent picture gallery. A detachment of princely grenadiers mounted guard at the palace gates.

Most important for the later direction of Haydn's career, the establishment also included an opera-house and a marionette theatre. The former, seating over 400 people, was described by one visiting English aristocrat as 'the most elegant and handsomest I ever saw', while the latter was built in the form of a grotto, its walls encrusted with stones and shells. Both buildings were to be inaugurated with performances of works by Haydn, and the opera-house was to become the focus of his life for more than a decade from the mid-1770s.

Eszterháza became the most enduring of the prince's obsessions. Originally intended as a summer retreat, it gradually established itself as the court's principal residence, with Nicolaus often spending at least nine months of the year there. In spite of this, and of the enormous care lavished on the princely quarters, the accommodation for the musicians was cramped and basic. Only a handful of leading members of the establishment were able to have their wives and families with them (including Haydn, who by now might have preferred not to) and many of the others were living two to a room – a situation which would prove the seedbed for one of Haydn's most famous symphonies.

As the years went by, Haydn was to feel above all the isolation of his life at Eszterháza. At the same time, he recognized the profound effect of that isolation on his creativity. In perhaps the most quoted of all his remarks, he told Griesinger:

> *My Prince was content with all my works, I received approval, I could, as head of an orchestra, make experiments, observe what enhanced an effect, and what weakened it, thus improving, adding to, cutting away, and running risks. I was set apart from the world, there was nobody in my vicinity to confuse and annoy me in my course, and so I had to be original.*

Haydn's early biographer, Giuseppe Carpani, expanded this famous summary with the following account of the composer's working methods on these remote Hungarian estates:

> *I know from certain of the musicians who lived with him at Eszterháza that frequently he interrupted his work, left his chamber, gathered the orchestra together, tried out one passage or another on different instruments, and, having made the experiment, returned to his worktable, and continued his composition with assurance.*

The effects of this new assurance were not slow in appearing.

STURM UND DRANG

It used to be conventional to speak of a 'romantic crisis' in Haydn's music in the years around 1770. This supposed crisis, sometimes linked to the composer's unhappy marital situation and a serious illness in 1770, used also to be regarded as part of the so-called *Sturm und Drang* ('Storm and Stress') movement, the first phase of Romanticism in German culture.

Certainly, the works Haydn produced from about 1766 to about 1772 mark a new departure. Certainly too, they represent a period of development in his musical thinking unparalleled in its intensity either before or afterwards. Indeed, it is no exaggeration to say that in these few years of dynamic exploration and advance, Haydn not only laid the foundation for the great works of his own maturity, but changed the whole direction of European music.

It would be wrong, however, to see this creative ferment as necessarily an outgrowth of his personal life. As we have seen, eighteenth-century composers regarded themselves first and foremost as craftsmen, producing music for social and religious occasions as circumstances and patrons required. The Romantic conception of music as an expression of the inner self would have been quite alien to Haydn and is altogether unilluminating as a means of appreciating his greatness (even were it possible to deduce neat cause-and-effect relationships between an artist's life and work).

Nor is the *Sturm und Drang* label more than a convenient shorthand. For one thing, the movement was principally a literary one (and Haydn, for all his musical sophistication, was a singularly unliterary man). For another, it took hold in Austria only after the end of Haydn's most intense period of development, and especially with the publication of Goethe's enormously influential novel *The Sorrows of Young Werther* in 1774. While the superficial similarities between what was happening in Haydn's music and what would shortly be happening in European literature are undoubtedly attractive, therefore, they are ultimately misleading. In particular, they take account of only one side – the darker, more dramatic, minor-mode side – of Haydn's multifaceted output during these remarkable years of transition.

It is especially in the three instrumental forms that would stand at the heart of the Viennese classical style – the symphony, the string quartet and the piano sonata – that one can see the revolutionary effect of Haydn's work in the early Eszterháza period. All emerge transformed from the crucible of his imagination. The gulf between *Symphony No.6* (*Le matin*) of 1761 and the C minor *Symphony No.52* of the early 1770s (one of the crowning works of the period of transition) is markedly wider than between the latter and Beethoven's great C minor symphony, the Fifth, of 1808. A new language was being forged, and it was Joseph Haydn, almost single-handedly, who was creating it. With *Le matin* we are within reach of the Baroque; with *Symphony No.52* we are on the threshold of the nineteenth century.

It is in the so-called *Sturm und Drang* symphonies that one sees the most dramatic birth-pangs of that new era. None of Haydn's previous works exhibits the passionate intensity of the *Lamentatione Symphony*, which embodies plainsong melodies in its first and second movements, or the profoundly tragic *La Passione* (No.49) in F minor (perhaps Haydn's most personal key). Again, a work such as the *Trauer* (Mourning) *Symphony* (No.44) – so called because the composer was said to have wanted the second movement played at his funeral – may still be a long way from the last great symphonies of the 1790s, but the musical language is recognizably that of the mature Haydn.

These are works of great variety, but common features can be found in many of them. They are almost all works of heightened drama and rigorous development. Nervous driving rhythms, irregular phrase lengths and disconcerting pauses abound. There is a preponderance of unison-writing in the opening themes (as in the first movements of Nos.44, 46 & 52), often allied to wide and jagged interval leaps. Sonata movements are increasingly monothematic, with the material growing from small distinctive motifs and development occurring throughout, rather than just in the development section proper. Counterpoint is woven even more tightly into the fabric of the music (for example in the finale of No.38, the slow movement of No.47, or the stark canonic minuets of the *Lamentatione* and *Trauer Symphonies*) and contributes significantly to the emotional tension. Indeed, intellect buttresses emotion throughout these works, and it is a tribute to Prince Nicolaus' musical connoisseurship that he was able to recognize their worth. Not every Enlightenment aristocrat, for example, would have appreciated the subtleties of the minuet and trio *al Roverso* of *Symphony No.47*, in which the first section of each is played (and orchestrated) backwards in the second. That Haydn was fully conscious of the extent to which he was stretching his listeners by such complexities can be seen in the simplifications he made in the slow movement of No.42, over which he wrote '*Dieses war vor gar zu gelehrte Ohren*' ('This was for far too learned ears').

Perhaps the most remarkable of all the symphonies of this period is also the best known – No.45, the *Farewell*. The nickname derives from the circumstances of its composition (in 1772), which have already been touched on in describing the musicians' accommodation at Eszterháza. Griesinger tells the story as Haydn relayed it to him:

> *In Prince Esterházy's orchestra were several vigorous young married men who in summer, when the Prince stayed at Eszterháza castle, had to leave their wives behind in Eisenstadt. Contrary to his custom the Prince once wished to extend his stay in Eszterháza by several weeks. The fond husbands, especially dismayed at this news, turned to Haydn and pleaded with him to do something.*
>
> *Haydn had the notion of writing a symphony . . . in which one instrument after the other is silent. This symphony was performed at the first opportunity in the presence of the Prince, and each of the musicians was directed, as soon as his part was finished, to put out his candle, pack up his music and, with his instrument under his arm, to go away. The Prince and the audience understood the meaning of this pantomime at once, and the next day came the order to depart from Eszterháza.*

It is a good joke, and one that speaks volumes for Haydn's relationship both with his musicians and his employer. But there is vastly more to the *Farewell Symphony* than that. It is formally the most innovative work of Haydn's most innovative period. For a start it is the only eighteenth-century symphony in the unusual key of F sharp minor – the Eszterháza blacksmith had to make new crooks for the horns before they could play it. The audacity of the harmonic language is evident even to the post-Romantic ear (as witness the jolting D natural in the opening bars of the minuet), and the gradual reduction of forces in the finale to two violins (played at the first performance by Tomasini and Haydn himself) is only the most conspicuous of its structural experiments. Above all, the symphony as a whole breathes an unforgettable air of unease bordering on desolation, an atmosphere that greatly affected Mendelssohn when he revived the work in Leipzig in 1838.

The late 1760s and early 1770s also found Haydn returning to the string quartet after almost a decade (the quartets Op.3, which include the popular '*Serenade*' once attributed to Haydn, are now known to have been written by a priest called Hofstetter). Between about 1768 and 1772, however, he produced eighteen new quartets, published in sets of six as Opp.9, 17 & 20. All represent a marked advance on the quartets of Opp.1 & 2; indeed, the *D minor Quartet* Op.9 No.4 is arguably the first masterpiece of the medium. But it is in the Op.20 works of 1772 that Haydn achieved in the string quartet a breakthrough comparable to, and perhaps of even greater significance than, the one he was realizing in the symphonies of the same period.

These quartets have been described by the eminent Haydn scholar H.C. Robbins Landon as the works in which the Viennese classical style arrived at its full maturity. For the first time the four instruments are genuine individuals concerted in perfect balance. In particular, the cello has found its independent voice, most confidently in the opening movement of No.2 in C major, where Haydn gives it the first statement of the theme. The quartets also represent a new watershed in the refinement of sonata principles, and the muscularity of their structural logic is gloriously evident throughout. In three of the quartets, the minuet and trio is placed second in the order of the four movements as a counterpoise to the new gravity of the slow movements, which are always deeply felt and often of luminous beauty. Three of the quartets conclude with fully realized fugues, which were much admired and imitated by Haydn's contemporaries, including Mozart. As in the symphonies of this period, one seems at times, especially in the *G minor Quartet* (No.3), already to hear the musical language of Beethoven, whose study of these works is attested by a surviving copy he made of No.1. The richness and variety of these six quartets continues to astonish after more than two centuries of musical evolution. As the great critic Sir Donald Tovey said of Op.20: 'There is perhaps no single . . . opus in the history of instrumental music which has achieved so much.'

In the piano sonatas of the late 1760s and early 1770s too, one can see the same remarkable development in Haydn's musical personality as informs the contemporary symphonies and string quartets. Bedevilled by uncertainties though the chronology of these works is, Haydn seems to have written some 26 sonatas during the decade from 1766, of which a number are lost. Of those that remain, one, *Sonata No.33 in C minor* (XVI:20), stands out as the first undisputed masterpiece of the genre, and was perhaps Haydn's first sonata for the piano rather than for harpsichord or clavier. Written in 1771 though not published until 1780, it shares many of the characteristics of the *Sturm und Drang* works and is positively symphonic in its breadth. The first movement welds numerous apparently heterogeneous motifs into a powerful unity; the slow movement provides a moment of repose which nonetheless explores sonorities at the extremes of the keyboard; while the finale is a frenetic sonata-rondo that builds to a passionate and technically demanding climax.

Although there are other groundbreaking sonatas from these transitional years – No.31 in A flat major (XVI:46), with its beautifully sustained slow movement, being among the most impressive – no other sonata of the time looks as far ahead as the C minor, and in those that followed there is a palpable sense of relaxation after the tremendous creative effort of the *Sturm und Drang*. The sonatas published in 1774 (Nos.36–41; XVI:21–26) and 1776 (Nos.42–47; XVI:27–32) are works of great charm and craftsmanship but have none of the questing spirit that informs Nos.31–33.

There is a similar easing of emotional tension in the symphonies of the same period. Superlatively crafted and full of memorable orchestral effects, symphonies such as No.55 (obscurely nicknamed the *Schoolmaster*) or No.68 in B flat, written in 1774 and 1774–75 respectively, are more comfortable pieces than the turbulent, often minor-mode, works of the immediately preceding period. As for the string quartet, after the intense productivity that gave birth to Opp.9, 17 & 20, it would be nine years before Haydn returned to the form.

LIFE AT ESZTERHÁZA

Astonishing as is the achievement represented by such works, they constitute only a part of the phenomenal activity, both musical and administrative, of Haydn's first Eszterháza decade. Composition of works for the prince's baryton continued unabated. Furthermore, the death of Werner brought church music within Haydn's professional ambit for the first time since his freelance years, and the late 1760s saw a tremendous flowering in his sacred compositions. These include the huge *Missa Cellensis in honorem Beatissimae Virginis Mariae* of 1766, a cantata-mass designed for the pilgrimage church of Mariazell which he had visited as a newly unemployed chorister in 1750; the 1767 *Stabat Mater*, the first of Haydn's sacred works to reach a broad European audience and one for which he was proud to receive the praise of the venerable operatic composer Johann Hasse; the *Missa in honorem Beatissimae Virgine Mariae* (*Great Organ Solo Mass*) of 1768–69; and the cantata *Applausus* of 1768.

In connection with the latter work, there is extant a fascinating letter from Haydn, who could not attend its first performance at Zwettl Abbey in Lower Austria, setting out in great detail how the work should be played. It is a fund of information about his performance practices and requirements, and bears witness to the extraordinary (and extraordinarily time-consuming) care he took over such matters. As well as urging the need for three or four rehearsals, he even reminds the copyist so to copy the violin parts as to avoid all the players having to turn their pages at the same time, which would diminish the orchestral sound.

Haydn himself was later to tell Griesinger that he didn't know how he had managed to compose as much as he did, given the other demands on his time, and those demands are only too apparent during these years of his most intense creative activity. His concern for the well-being of the musicians in his care, which was to earn him the enduring epithet of 'Papa' Haydn, is never more evident than now. The Esterházy archives contain numerous letters of intercession on behalf of suppliant or wayward employees, including one relating to an unedifying incident in which the cellist blinded the oboist in one eye during a pub brawl in 1771. To modern ears the tone of these essays in persuasive diplomacy is one of extreme subservience, of which the following, from a letter to Prince Nicolaus of December 1766, is a typical sample:

The most joyous occasion of your name-day ... obliges me not only to deliver to you in profound submission 6 new divertimenti, but also to say that we were delighted to receive, a few days ago, our new Winter clothes – and submissively to kiss the hem of your robe for this especial act of kindness. . . . Incidentally, the two oboe players report (and I myself must agree with them) that their oboes are so old that they are collapsing, and no longer keep the proper pitch; for this reason I would humbly point out to YOUR HIGHNESS that there is a master Rockobauer in Vienna, who in my opinion is the most skilful for this sort of work. But . . . the cheapest price is 8 ducats. I therefore await YOUR HIGHNESS' gracious consent whether the above-mentioned and most urgently needed two oboes may be constructed for the price indicated. I hope for your favour and grace.

No less remarkable than the minutiae with which a composer of Haydn's standing was expected to deal, of course, is the fact that one of the greatest princes of the Habsburg empire, with more than a million acres of land under his control, should concern himself with the price of his musicians' oboes. The other side of the same coin, however, is the paternalistic care with which, when a fire devastated Eisenstadt in 1768, destroying the composer's home and numerous musical scores, Esterházy had Haydn's house rebuilt at his own expense, and was happy to loan his *Kapellmeister* 400 gulden to repay an earlier mortgage on the property a couple of years later.

If long stretches of Haydn's life at Eszterháza were undoubtedly mundane and monotonous, it was also punctuated by spectacular festivities of the kind that helped to earn Prince Nicolaus his epithet 'the Magnificent'. Celebrations of family events and anniversaries, or receptions for visiting dignitaries, these invariably involved Haydn in major musical commissions (and considerable extra administrative work). In the summer of 1766, for example, he wrote the *intermezzo* (comic opera) *La canterina* (The singing girl) for the name-day of Nicolaus' son and heir, Anton; while in 1770 he 'had the honour to receive the most flattering praise from all the illustrious guests' for his opera *Le pescatrici* (The fisherwomen), produced to celebrate the marriage of the prince's niece. Again, in 1775, a visit from the Archduke Ferdinand and his consort prompted the composition of Haydn's 'Turkish' opera *L'incontro improvviso* (The unforeseen encounter) as part of an extravaganza that also included a huge masked ball;

a performance of the play *Le distrait* (The distracted man), from his incidental music to which Haydn quarried the whirling agglomeration of folk-tunes which is his *Symphony No.60* (*Il distratto*); an all-night illumination of the Eszterháza grounds; and a feudalistic rally of 2,000 Hungarian and Croatian peasants singing ethnic folksongs.

Perhaps the most memorable of all these festivities, however, were those for the two-day state visit of the Empress Maria Theresa in September 1773. The centrepiece of the proceedings was a performance of Haydn's opera *L'infedeltà delusa* (Infidelity outwitted), which had been premiered earlier in the year at the almost equally opulent celebrations for the Dowager Duchess Esterházy's name-day and which is often regarded as dramatically his most successful stage work. Despite its anti-aristocratic subtext, it seems to have impressed the Empress too: she is said to have told her Viennese circle that if she wanted to hear a good opera she went to Eszterháza – a claim that might have carried more weight had she ever visited the palace again!

There was also a concert in the Chinese pavilion, at which Haydn and his musicians performed in oriental dress. It used to be thought that the programme included the *Symphony No.48*, one of the most exhilarating of Haydn's lifelong series of festive C major symphonies, and still known as the *Maria Theresa* on that account. Since this was written in 1769, however, it seems more likely that the newly-composed *Symphony No.50*, also in C major, was the one the Empress actually heard. The following day the marionette theatre was officially opened with a performance of Haydn's marionette opera *Philemon und Baucis*, one of only two of his works in the genre to have survived. When the composer was presented to Maria Theresa, he took the opportunity to remind her of the thrashing she had ordered when he was caught climbing on the scaffolding at Schönbrunn as a choirboy almost thirty years before.

As these various festivities show, opera – both at the marionette theatre and at the opera-house, which had been inaugurated in 1768 with Haydn's comic opera *Lo speziale* (The apothecary) – was already an important focus of musical activity at Eszterháza. Indeed, the growing demands of operatic performance and composition may well be one of the reasons why the works immediately following the *Sturm und Drang* years so often fail to match the emotional energy of their predecessors.

In 1776, however, the prince instituted a major change in the pattern of musical life in his court with the introduction of a regular opera season at Eszterháza. The effects of this change were to determine the direction of Haydn's career for the next decade.

CHAPTER 5

THE OPERA YEARS
(1776–85)

- ◆ Haydn's operas
- ◆ The opera director
- ◆ Growing popularity

H aydn, like most eighteenth-century composers, regarded the writing of operas as central to his musical life. In the biographical sketch he wrote in 1776, he lists three operas and two sacred works as his most successful up to that time, making no mention of his numerous symphonies, quartets, trios or piano sonatas, and in the mid-1780s he seems to have shared his employer's view that the now almost wholly forgotten *dramma eroico Armida* was the best thing he'd ever written.

It is all the more remarkable, therefore, that today most people barely think of Haydn as an operatic composer at all. None of his numerous operas has a regular place in the modern repertoire, although some have been revived in recent years, and there is still only one representative series of recordings. Why should this be?

HAYDN'S OPERAS
Haydn himself believed that his operas were too tailored to the performing conditions at Eszterháza for them to do justice to themselves elsewhere. In a famous letter to one Franz Roth in Prague in 1787, he wrote:

> You ask me for an opera buffa. Most willingly, if you want to have one of my vocal compositions for yourself alone. But if you intend to produce it on the stage at Prague, in that case I cannot

> *comply with your wish, because all my operas are far too closely*
> *connected with our personal circle (Esterház* [sic] *in Hungary),*
> *and moreover they would not produce the proper effect, which*
> *I calculated in accordance with the locality.*

There is no doubt some truth in this. At the same time, it is true of most pre-Romantic music, and perhaps especially of opera, that it was created with specific occasions and venues in mind, and no such constraints have prevented the operas of Gluck or Mozart from remaining in the repertoire.

The mention of Haydn's younger contemporary provides perhaps a more significant clue to the meteoric decline of Haydn's operas into the obscurity in which they still languish today. Indeed, the letter to Roth goes on to say:

> *It would be quite another matter if I were to have the great*
> *good fortune to compose a brand new libretto for your theatre.*
> *But even then I should be risking a good deal, for scarcely any*
> *man can brook comparison with the great Mozart.*

Over no other category of Haydn's work does the shadow of Mozart hang so heavily as over his operas. Listening to *L'infedeltà delusa* or *L'incontro improvviso*, both written more than a decade before Mozart began his great collaboration with the librettist Lorenzo Da Ponte, one is continually reminded of the younger composer, and it is impossible to avoid precisely the comparisons Haydn himself knew he could not sustain.

L'incontro improvviso, the plot of which is so strikingly similar to that of Mozart's own 'Turkish' opera, *Die Entführung aus dem Serail* (The abduction from the harem), is perhaps particularly handicapped in this respect. It deploys, albeit sparingly, the same battery of quasi-Ottoman percussion; it even has a bluff bass servant called Osmin. As in Haydn's other mature works for the stage, there is no shortage of fine individual numbers, from the broad comic songs of Osmin and Calandro to the tender love duet '*Son quest'occhi*' of Ali and Rezia (sung at the first performance by Karl Friberth, who also adapted the libretto, and his wife Magdalena, whom we last met as the baby whose birth forced Haydn to leave his first lodgings in Vienna so many years before). The greatest single number, the breathtaking soprano *terzetto*, '*Mi sembra un sogno*' in Act 1, prompts comparison with the famous Act 1 trio '*Soave sia il vento*' from Mozart's *Così fan tutte*. The problem, however, as so often in Haydn's operas, is that these individual numbers do not add up to a dramatic whole greater than the sum of its parts.

If this is partly due to the librettos Haydn set, it is also true that he seems to have been markedly less critical in his choice and adaptation of texts than Mozart, who was notoriously taxing in the demands he made of his librettists. Nor does Haydn often infuse his characters with the depth of humanity that Mozart is able to find even in his stock types and villains – though there are certainly moments, such as Filippo's sudden compassion for Nencio's supposedly deserted wife and children in the midst of his aria of outrage in Act II of *L'infedeltà delusa*, or Sandrina's heartfelt aria '*È la pompa un grand'imbroglio*' in the same work, when the stereotypes of Italian comic opera suddenly take on the emotional contours of real life. It is moments like these that make one wonder how Haydn's operas, with their wealth of glorious music and their magnificent set-pieces, would now be placed in the history of the form had Mozart never written for the stage.

Whatever the reasons for the failure of Haydn's operas yet to have reasserted their hold on the imagination of the concert-going public, the writing of them was one of his major compositional tasks at both Eisenstadt and Eszterháza and occupied a vast amount of his creative energy up to 1783. By the time Prince Nicolaus instituted the regular operatic season at Eszterháza in 1776, Haydn had already written more than a dozen operas, *Singspiele* and marionette operas in his service, though a number of these are now completely or partially lost. For at least the next decade opera was, in one form or another, to consume so much of his professional time as to displace almost everything else.

THE OPERA DIRECTOR

Until 1776 the theatre at Eszterháza had mainly been used for plays performed by visiting troupes of actors, who would be signed up for the whole summer season. One of the Prince's favourite troupes was the one led by the celebrated actor-manager Carl Wahr, who was instrumental in introducing the plays of Shakespeare to the German-speaking countries, and is known to have performed *Hamlet*, *King Lear* and *Macbeth* at Eszterháza. The core of his repertoire, however, was comic and Haydn may well have written more incidental music for such performances than has come down to us. Operas, on the other hand, were mounted principally for the kind of special occasions already described, and were specifically written for them by Haydn himself.

From 1776, however, opera increasingly took centre stage. Never a man to do things by halves, Prince Nicolaus proceeded to invest in his new love all the reserves of energy (not to mention money) that he had previously channelled into his baryton. He acquired numerous opera scores, especially by contemporary Italian composers, and took on new singers to perform them. In the first full season of the new regime five operas were given, one by Sacchini, one by Piccinni, and three by the newly-ennobled Ditters von Dittersdorf, whom Haydn had known and drunk with as plain Karl Ditters in his freelance days in Vienna. Ten years later, in 1786, an astonishing seventeen operas were performed during the year, nine of which were new to the repertoire – a grand total of some 125 performances in a single season. The average annual number was somewhere between these two extremes. In other words, for much of the late 1770s and 1780s there were opera nights at Eszterháza two or three times a week during a season that sometimes lasted as long as eleven months.

Haydn was responsible for all these performances. The administrative workload was immense. Quite apart from directing the performances themselves, he had to arrange and supervise everything from the copying of the material to the rehearsing of singers and orchestra. In addition, he had to adapt existing material to the demands of the Eszterháza opera-house, which often involved a radical overhaul of the original scores. While such adaptations were common practice in the eighteenth century, Haydn seems to have been characteristically thoroughgoing – not to say ruthless – in his approach to the task, not only making cuts and rearrangements as required to suit the forces under his direction, but also writing numerous new arias, and even duets and *terzettos*, for insertion into other composers' works. In addition, he continued to compose and mount operas of his own for Prince Nicolaus until 1784, when he produced *Armida*, his last opera for the Esterházy family. In short, his job had changed almost overnight to that of opera director, to which role his duties as composer quickly became subordinate.

The catalogue of works directed by Haydn at Eszterháza represents an illuminating index of aristocratic taste in opera in the 1770s and 1780s. It seems reasonable to assume that the six operas Haydn composed during the same period also reflect Prince Nicolaus' preferences. These seem to have been for comic operas with increasingly heroic overtones, though Haydn calls only one, *Orlando Paladino* (1782), a *dramma eroi-comico*. Those that precede it – *Il mondo della luna* (1777), *La vera costanza* (1778), *L'isola disabitata* (1779) and *La fedeltà premiata* (1780) – are each called *dramma giocoso* (the same designation Mozart was to use for *Don Giovanni*). After *Orlando Paladino* the prince seems to have developed a taste for fully-fledged *opera seria*, and Haydn's last opera for the Eszterháza opera-house, *Armida* (1783, performed 1784), is designated a *dramma eroico*.

Il mondo della luna (The world of the moon), written in 1777 for the wedding festivities of the prince's second son Count Nicolaus and the Countess von Weissenwolf, is the last of Haydn's operas in which the *buffo* elements are predominant. It is a delightful farce, with a libretto based on a play by the renowned Italian playwright Carlo Goldoni, who had also provided the texts for Haydn's earlier operas *Lo speziale* and *Le pescatrici*. The story concerns a bogus astronomer, Ecclitico, who hoodwinks a gullible old man, Buonafede, into thinking he has been transported to the moon. The finale to Act II is a masterpiece of gathering tension, but the finest number is unquestionably the love-duet between Ecclitico and Buonafede's daughter Clarice (*'Un certo ruscelletto'*), which is the centrepiece of the short third act. Haydn later reworked the overture as the first movement of *Symphony No.63* (*La Roxolane*). Ernesto's Act II aria *'Qualche volta non fa male'* (on the benefits of severity towards women!) reappears in a more unlikely guise as the Benedictus of the 1782 *Missa Cellensis* or *Mariazell Mass* (XXII:8), the only major sacred work of Haydn's operatic years and the last piece of church music he would write until he began his final great series of masses in 1796.

The following two years saw the composition of two new operas, both more serious in tone than *Il mondo della luna*: *La vera costanza* (True constancy) and *L'isola disabitata* (The desert island), the latter to a libretto by his old master of the Michaelerhaus, Pietro Metastasio. Both were performed during the 1779 season, which also saw the production of Haydn's last marionette opera *Die bestrafte Rachbegierde*, now lost, as well as the usual quota of operas by other composers. To compound the pressure of this daunting schedule, Haydn also had to contend with the effects of a major fire, which had gutted the opera-house in November, destroying among other things a number of scores and Haydn's harpsichord, and necessitated the transfer of operatic productions to the marionette theatre. The construction of a new opera-house began the following month, and Haydn wrote his magnificent *Symphony No. 70*, with its massive contrapuntal finale on an eerie five-note motto, to celebrate the laying of the foundation stone.

1779 was a significant year for Haydn in other respects too. In March an Italian violinist, Antonio Polzelli, and his much younger wife Luigia, a soprano, joined the Esterházy musical establishment. Both were mediocre musicians, but Haydn seems to have been instrumental in overturning the notice of dismissal that came their way in 1780. The reason was that by then Luigia had become his mistress. Now in his late forties, Haydn clearly felt a need for the affection his marriage had failed to provide (not least after what was almost certainly his wife's affair with the artist Ludwig Guttenbrunn, whose 1770 visit to Eszterháza has left us a strikingly self-confident image of Haydn as a thirty-eight-year-old *Kapellmeister*). Many of Haydn's insertion arias and operatic rearrangements were designed to accommodate Luigia Polzelli's limited talents. There is also good reason to believe that he was the father of her son Alois, known as 'Antonio' (born 1783), who went on to become a musician himself. As late as May 1800, two months after his wife's death, we find Haydn signing an extraordinary undertaking 'to *Signora* Loisa [*sic*] Polzelli (in case I should consider marrying again) to take no wife other than said Loisa Polzelli, and should I remain a widower, I promise said Polzelli to leave her, after my death, a pension for life of three hundred Gulden'. Luigia subsequently married an Italian singer.

Also in 1779, Haydn was involved in a bitter altercation with the Tonkünstlersocietät of Vienna, a benevolent society founded to assist musicians and their dependants, for whose benefit he had fulfilled his first Viennese commission since *Der krumme Teufel* with his oratorio *Il ritorno di Tobia* in 1775. In 1778 Haydn had applied for membership of the society, with the required registration fee for an out-of-town member, but in January 1779 heard that the society would only accept him if he undertook to compose major works for their benefit concerts on demand – a proviso that ran counter to the terms of his contract with the Esterházy family and, as Haydn put it with uncharacteristically Romantic passion, to the principle that 'the fine arts, and such a wonderful science as that of composition allow no gyves on their handicraft.' To their discredit, the society accepted Haydn's angry withdrawal.

A third significant development in 1779 was the revision of Haydn's contract of employment with Prince Nicolaus. The new agreement was a more even-handed document than its predecessor – for example both parties now had to give three months notice of termination to the other – and reflected the confidence that had grown up between the prince and his *Kapellmeister* over almost two decades. The most important change, other than an increase in salary and benefits that made Haydn one of the highest paid employees in the entire court, was the omission of the exclusivity clause that had bound him to compose only for his employer unless granted permission to the contrary. Even though the original clause had been interpreted with some flexibility in practice, especially in recent years, its formal removal opened the way for Haydn to capitalize on a reputation that was already spreading rapidly outside the narrow confines of the Esterházy court. Indeed, in the following year, 1780, he began one of the most important business associations of his career with the leading Viennese musical publishers Artaria & Co., who in April published his six piano sonatas Nos.48–52 and 33 (XVI:35–39 and 20). From this point forward, his compositions were increasingly to be written for publication.

Meanwhile, however, opera continued to demand Haydn's almost undivided attention. The new opera-house was opened, a little later than expected, in 1781 with a performance of *La fedeltà premiata* (Fidelity rewarded), musically the finest of Haydn's operas and the centrepiece of this period of his creative life. The sub-classical plot may require a more than usually determined suspension of disbelief, but the arias of Celia, Amaranta and Fileno contain some of Haydn's most enchanting music, and the monumental chain-finales to Acts I and II are miraculously sustained, both musically and dramatically. Haydn later remarshalled the rollicking overture as the finale to *Symphony No. 73* (*La chasse*).

The following year saw the premiere of *Orlando Paladino*, an adaptation of the chivalric tale of Ariosto's hero Orlando, and a work on the border of *opera seria*, which Haydn would formally cross with his last opera for Eszterháza, *Armida*, which was premiered in 1784 and repeated no less than 45 times up to the end of 1786.

GROWING POPULARITY

Given the amount of creative energy he was having to channel into opera, not to mention the fact that his directorial function alone was by modern standards a full-time job, it is amazing that Haydn managed to write any other music at all during these years. Certainly, there is a marked decline in his productivity outside opera in the decade or so to about 1785. Moreover, his contributions to the categories of work that had always been at the forefront of his musical development – most notably the symphony – are, at least by Haydn's exalted standards, less distinguished during this period than at any other. At the same time, many of the symphonies from these years were among his most popular during his lifetime. No.53 (*L'Impériale*), for example, written around 1777, remained a favourite work with eighteenth-century audiences throughout Europe. It brought the house down in the London concert season of 1781 and the slow movement was engraved on the statue Count Harrach erected at Rohrau in Haydn's honour in 1793.

Similarly, the two sets of symphonies Nos.76–78 and 79–81 – significantly enough, his first to be composed with an eye to international publication – were popular in intention as well as in effect: writing to music publishers in Paris in 1783, Haydn said of the first set: 'Last year I composed 3 beautiful, elegant and by no means over-lengthy Symphonies, scored for 2 violins, viola, basso, 2 horns, 2 oboes, 1 flute and 1 bassoon – but they are all very easy, and without too much *concertante*. . . . ' These are not terms one could ever use of the revolutionary symphonies of the late 1760s and early 1770s.

Again, the six Op.33 string quartets of 1781 (published 1782), his first since the groundbreaking Op.20 set almost a decade earlier, are more a consolidation of his achievement in the form than the new departure implied by Haydn's own description of them as being 'written in a new and special way'. This much quoted phrase occurs in what are effectively marketing letters to potential subscribers and is surely more significant as an index of Haydn's newly-found commercial confidence than as stylistic analysis. Sometimes known as the 'Russian' quartets because of their dedication to the Grand Duke Paul of Russia, whose wife was probably a pupil of Haydn's and for whose projected visit to Eszterháza in 1781 *Orlando Paladino* had originally been written, the Op.33 quartets contain some of Haydn's finest writing, and were highly influential (most notably on the 26-year-old Mozart, who encountered them shortly after launching himself on his freelance career in Vienna in 1782). The second quartet in the series is known as the *Joke*, because Haydn tricks the listener into thinking the finale is over four times before it actually ends. The third quartet, known as the *Bird* after the chirruping themes of the opening movement, is perhaps the finest of the set, its second movement (*scherzando allegretto*) making C major sound as dark-toned as a minor key by exploiting the instruments' lowest strings.

This period also saw the composition of two of Haydn's best-known concertos, his second surviving *Cello Concerto* (VIIb:2) in D, and the *Piano Concerto in D* (VIII:11). The latter is far the most frequently performed of Haydn's piano concertos, a medium in which, as in opera, his achievement has been overshadowed by that of Mozart; it is particularly notable for the beauty of its slow movement and for its spectacular finale, a '*Rondo all'Ungherese*' in which Haydn's intermittent flirtation with gypsy music over the years explodes into a whirling Hungarian (or more probably Bosnian-Dalmatian) dance, bringing us close to the sound world of Liszt's Hungarian rhapsodies.

Although he continued to be actively involved in the direction of opera at Eszterháza until 1790 – as we have seen, 1786 was his busiest operatic year of all – Haydn ceased composing operas himself for Prince Nicolaus after 1784. Since this had been his chief remaining compositional duty at Eszterháza, and since he was no longer bound by the exclusivity clause of his 1761 contract, in the mid-1780s Haydn found himself, for the first time in his mature career, free to direct his formidable creative energies elsewhere than to the service of his prince. It is a tribute to Haydn's sheer stamina that, in his early fifties, effectively a full-time opera director and with a quarter of a century of unremitting musical activity behind him, he was able to take advantage of that freedom. That he was able to do so with the enhanced creative vigour that would, during his remaining years of active life, give birth to his greatest masterpieces is little short of miraculous.

Even as his last two Esterházy operas, *Orlando Paladino* and *Armida*, were enjoying the longest success of any of his stage works at Eszterháza, the first fruits of that freedom were already ripening. Around the beginning of 1785 Haydn had received from a Paris-based concert organization, Le Concert de la Loge Olympique, a request for six symphonies. It was Haydn's first major foreign commission and a milestone on his road to unprecedented international fame.

CHAPTER 6
AN INTERNATIONAL REPUTATION
(1786–90)

♦ *'Loved in the whole of Europe'*
♦ *'My misfortune is that I live in the country'*
♦ *Haydn and Mozart*

S lowly but inexorably, throughout his years as *Kapellmeister* to the Esterházys, Haydn's reputation had been seeping out into the wider musical world from the isolated environment of Prince Nicolaus' court.

Griesinger tells us that, remote from the musical mainstream as he was in the Hungarian marshlands of the Neusiedlersee, for a long time Haydn 'did not know himself how celebrated he was abroad, and he heard of it only occasionally from travelling foreigners who visited him'.

By the 1780s, however, his reputation had gained sufficient momentum throughout Europe for him to have begun to realize its strength even in the closed circle of Eszterháza. This realization is reflected in the self-confident tone of his letters to Artaria and other publishers. One cannot imagine the younger Haydn, for example, writing as he did to Artaria in 1781: 'If they [the French] only could hear my operetta [*sic*] *L'isola disabitata* and my most recent opera, *La fedeltà premiata*, I assure you that no such work has been heard in Paris up to now, nor perhaps in Vienna either.'

That this new-found awareness of his fame was also starting to make him restless for that wider world can be seen in the phrase immediately following the sentence just quoted: 'my misfortune is that I live in the country'. That restlessness, and in particular a yearning for the cosmopolitan musical life of Vienna, was to become increasingly hard to bear over the next few years.

'LOVED IN THE WHOLE OF EUROPE'

As early as 1764 the first of a stream of pirated works – the string quartets Op.1 Nos.1–4 – had found their way to music publishers in France, where they were enthusiastically received. They were quickly followed by symphonies, string trios and numerous other works. Indeed, the market for music by Haydn was so buoyant in Paris and the French provinces that at least as many spurious as genuine works were published in France over the next 15 years. When they couldn't find enough genuine Haydn, publishers simply took manuscripts by other Austrian and German composers, such as his brother Michael, his friend Dittersdorf and his followers Vanhal, Pleyel and Ordoñez, and printed them under Haydn's name. In the absence of copyright laws, and with a community of professional music copyists given to hawking round the works they were supposed to be copying, the composer himself made no money at all from this burgeoning Haydn industry in what was then the musical capital of Europe.

Nor was it only in France that his reputation already stood high. In 1779 a Spanish poet called Yriarte had devoted a large section of his poem *La musica* to a panegyric on Haydn, and Spain was to be an important source of commissions over the coming years. Again, in 1781 Haydn had opened negotiations with music publishers in England, a country that was to take him to its heart a decade later and where his music was already enormously popular. Concert-promoters made attempts to lure him to London throughout the 1780s, and the newspaper which in 1785 described him as 'the Shakespeare of music, and the triumph of the age in which we live' was merely echoing the prevailing view in the city's musical circles at the time.

Haydn's music had been circulating in the Habsburg lands from the 1750s, often by dissemination through the great monasteries and mainly in manuscript. In 1774, despite the exclusivity clause of his original contract with Esterházy, his six piano sonatas Nos.36–41 (XVI:21–26) were published in Vienna with a dedication to Prince Nicolaus, and in 1775, as we have seen, came his first commission from Vienna since his freelance days, the oratorio *Il ritorno di Tobia*. One review of the oratorio's performance called Haydn 'the great artist . . . whose works are loved in the whole of Europe and in which foreigners find the original genius of a master' and reported that 'his choruses glowed with a fire that was otherwise only in Händel [*sic*]'. In 1776 he was considered famous enough to be featured in a who's who of the Austrian cultural scene, for which he wrote the autobiographical sketch already mentioned, and five years later, his Viennese publishers, Artaria, included his portrait in a gallery of leading figures in Austrian public life.

Perhaps the most remarkable feature of this snowballing celebrity was that it had come about without any help from the composer himself until he was almost fifty. Not only did Haydn live in physical and cultural isolation for most of the time his reputation was spreading; until he began his relationship with Artaria in 1780 there was also no publicity machine promoting his music for him. It had simply struck a chord in almost every part of Europe where it had been heard, and the musical public wanted more of it.

Prominent among that wider public was the Comte d'Ogny, a charismatic French aristocrat who was to become one of Haydn's most important foreign patrons. The count was the moving force behind the Concert de la Loge Olympique and was thus responsible for commissioning the six so-called '*Paris*' *Symphonies* (Nos.82–87). He paid the composer the handsome sum of 25 *louis d'or* per symphony for writing them, plus five *louis d'or* for the publication rights (though Haydn, who shared the publishing ethics of his age, also sold them to Artaria and his London publisher William Forster, as well as sending them to King Frederick William II of Prussia, the dedicatee of the six Op.50 quartets, who sent him a valuable ring in return). Three of the symphonies seem to have been written in 1785, the remaining three the following year. The first performances took place in Paris in 1787 and were greeted by ecstatic reviews. Despite his remoteness from the cultural life of the French capital, Haydn had proved uncannily adept at judging its taste.

The '*Paris*' *Symphonies* mark the beginning of that remarkable late flowering of Haydn's symphonic genius, which was to reach its apogee in the 12 '*London*' *Symphonies* of the 1790s. Among the most frequently performed of the composer's symphonies, they are wholly characteristic of Haydn's mature genius in their sturdy charm, their rich orchestral colours, and the concentration of their musical thinking. Three (Nos.84, 85 and 86) begin with the slow introduction that was to become a hallmark of the '*London*' *Symphonies*. No.82 has been nicknamed *L'ours* (The bear) because of the drone-bass below the main theme of the finale, which is supposedly reminiscent of a dancing bear's hurdy-gurdy music. Similarly, No.83 has the sobriquet *La poule* (The hen) for the clucking theme that forms the second subject of the first movement and which contrasts so effectively with the dramatic G minor opening subject. No.85 has, since its first publication in 1788, been known as *La Reine*, the queen in question being the ill-fated Marie-Antoinette, one of whose favourite pieces it was (and whose name reminds us that, for all the apparent changelessness of the social milieu for which Haydn was writing, we are now on the very threshold of the French Revolution). An unusual feature of the first movement of *La Reine* is Haydn's near-quotation of the opening theme of his *Farewell Symphony* of 1772. One French critic astutely remarked of these symphonies that Haydn could do more with a single theme than most contemporary composers could do with a profusion of them.

As Haydn was completing the '*Paris*' *Symphonies* he received from Cádiz one of his most unusual commissions, and one that would produce a work unique of its kind. This was *The Seven Last Words of Our Saviour on the Cross*, which was to be the centrepiece of the Good Friday ceremonies at Santa Cueva, a church built in a grotto near the city. The work is a series of seven slow movements for orchestra, each illustrative of one of Jesus' last pronouncements from the cross, together with an introduction and a fiery concluding movement, *Terremoto*, which depicts the earthquake following his death. Griesinger describes the impressive circumstances of its first performance:

> *On the appointed day the walls, windows, and piers of the church were draped with black, and only a single lamp of good size, hanging in the middle, illuminated the sacred darkness. At an appointed hour all doors were locked and the music began. After a suitable prelude the bishop mounted to the pulpit, pronounced one of the Seven Words, and delivered a meditation upon it. As soon as it was ended, he descended from the pulpit and knelt down before the altar. The music filled in this pause.*

The bishop entered the pulpit a second, a third time, and so on, and each time the orchestra came in again at the end of the talk.

Haydn himself, in the notes from which Griesinger drew this account, admitted that 'it was no easy task to compose seven adagios lasting ten minutes each, and to succeed one another without fatiguing the listeners; indeed, I found it quite impossible to confine myself to the appointed limits.' Certainly, there is nothing else quite like *The Seven Last Words* in the classical canon, and even today the work, which lasts more than an hour, demands (and repays) extreme concentration in the listening. It was, nonetheless, an immediate success and, together with the *'Paris' Symphonies*, gave Haydn's European reputation a significant boost. The composer himself regarded it as one of his most successful compositions, producing a choral version and a version for string quartet, and it was one of the works that was to remain in the repertoire throughout the nineteenth-century downturn in Haydn's reputation.

As if the *'Paris' Symphonies* and *The Seven Last Words* were not sufficient work for a year that was, as we have seen, Haydn's busiest as an opera director at Eszterháza, 1786 also saw him fulfilling a commission from another foreign patron, the eccentric King Ferdinand IV of Naples. Just as Prince Nicolaus had a passion for the baryton, so Ferdinand loved the even more esoteric *lira organizzata*, in effect a sophisticated form of hurdy-gurdy, and he approached Haydn to write him five concertos for two *lire organizzate*, strings and horns (VIIh:1–5). The king was so pleased with the results that he commissioned (about 1790) a further set of eight *notturni* (nocturnes) for two *lire organizzate*, clarinets, horns, violas and bass (II:25–32). Haydn later rescored these fine chamber works for more generally available forces, and also redeployed movements from the concertos in his *Symphonies Nos.89* and *100* (*Military*). All in all, there can be few more striking instances of the multifaceted nature of Haydn's gifts than the compositions of 1785 and 1786.

The following year, 1787, saw the composition of the so-called *'Tost' Symphonies*, Nos.88 and 89. Like their six illustrious predecessors, these were written for the Parisian market, and it is ironic that they have immortalized the name of the less than reliable intermediary, Johann Tost, a violinist in the Esterházy orchestra, to whom Haydn entrusted them, together with the six quartets now known as Opp.54 and 55, when the latter visited the French capital that year. To put it at its most charitable, Tost exceeded his brief: in addition to selling the two symphonies to a publisher as Haydn had wished, he also passed off another composer's symphony as Haydn's own and negotiated without Haydn's permission the sale of six of his piano sonatas! The whole affair cost Haydn much paper, ink and precious time in the unravelling. (The fact that three years later he was to dedicate to Tost one of his greatest sets of string quartets – the magnificent Op.64 – is yet another example of Haydn's easy-going nature.)

The *Symphony No.88* is one of Haydn's finest achievements in the form, and a classic example of his ability to combine the popular and the 'learned' in a single work. On hearing the beautiful slow movement, Brahms is reputed to have said that he wanted his ninth symphony to sound like that. The third movement is a particularly uplifting example of the celebratory peasant strain in Haydn's kaleidoscopically varied minuets, while from the last movement, with its instantly memorable theme, it is a small step to the finale of Beethoven's *First Symphony*, written twelve years later.

In 1788 – the year Mozart wrote his last three symphonies – the Comte d'Ogny commissioned Haydn to write another three symphonies for the Concert de la Loge Olympique. Since Haydn had recently received a commission for three symphonies from another of his foreign admirers, the south-German prince Krafft Ernst von Oettingen-Wallerstein, he took the opportunity to kill two birds with one stone by providing both patrons with the same set of symphonies, Nos.90–92. Whatever the commercial morality of the manoeuvre, the resulting works include, in No.92, one of Haydn's greatest symphonies. Known as the '*Oxford*' because it was the work played when the composer received his honorary doctorate in music from the University of Oxford in 1791, it is the last of Haydn's symphonies before the final twelve '*London*' *Symphonies* of the 1790s.

'MY MISFORTUNE IS THAT I LIVE IN THE COUNTRY'

The late 1780s were a time of revolutionary change not only in the European social and political arena but also in Haydn's personal and professional life. In 1790, the year after the French

Revolution, an epoch in Haydn's own career was to end with the death of the prince he had served for almost thirty years and the consequent disbanding of the Esterházy musical establishment. Furthermore, in the immediately preceding years Haydn had made two of the most important friendships of his life, both of which were transforming experiences and gave him still greater cause to feel his isolation from the cultural life of Vienna. One of these Viennese friends was Marianne von Genzinger, the wife of Prince Nicolaus' personal doctor. The other was Wolfgang Amadeus Mozart.

When she first wrote to Haydn in 1789, sending him a piano arrangement she had made of the slow movement of one of his symphonies, Marianne von Genzinger was thirty-nine, an accomplished musician and one of Vienna's most cultivated aristocratic hostesses. In the ensuing correspondence, which continued until Marianne's death in 1793, Haydn reveals more of himself than in any of his other surviving letters, and we have a keen sense of his having found at last a true confidante and, in the Genzinger family circle, something of the home life his own marriage had failed to provide. Speaking of his 'frequent depressed moods', he describes himself as 'a man who values you above everything else' and who fears 'losing even a fraction of your favour'. 'Your pleasant letters,' he says, ' . . . comfort me in my wilderness, and are highly necessary for my heart, which is often so deeply hurt,' and he longs to 'pour forth all my troubles to you, and to hear your comforting words.' He clearly spent as much time as possible at the Genzingers' house whenever he was in Vienna, and his letters paint an affecting contrast between his life in the capital and the 'dreary solitude' of Eszterháza. Most frequently quoted is the letter of 9 February 1790, perhaps the most personal document Haydn ever wrote, in which he laments his return to Eszterháza after one such visit:

> *Well, here I sit in my wilderness – forsaken – like a poor waif – almost without any human society – melancholy – full of the memories of past glorious days – yes! past alas! – and who knows when these days will return again? Those wonderful parties? Where the whole circle is one heart, one soul – all these beautiful musical evenings – which can only be remembered, and not described – where are all those enthusiastic moments? – all gone – and gone*

for a long time. Your grace mustn't be surprised that I haven't written up to now to thank you. I found everything at home in confusion, and for 3 days I didn't know if I was Capell-master *or* Capell- servant. *Nothing could console me, my whole house was in confusion, my pianoforte which I usually love so much was perverse and disobedient, it irritated rather than calmed me, and I could sleep only very little, even my dreams persecuted me; and then, just when I was happily dreaming that I was listening to the opera,* Le nozze di Figaro *, that horrible North wind woke me and almost blew my nightcap off my head.*

... Here in Estoras [Eszterháza] no one asks me: Would you like some chocolate, with milk or without? Will you take some coffee, black, or with cream? What may I offer you, my dear Haydn? ... I am gradually getting used to country life, however, and yesterday I studied for the first time, and quite Haydnish, too. ...

The same mood of wistful longing permeates such contemporaneous works as the slow movements of the fifth *lire organizzate* nocturne (II:27) and the *String Quartet in B minor* Op.64 No.2.

Haydn's frustration with life at Eszterháza became more acute as the attractions of Vienna became more personal. But it remained difficult for him to get permission to leave Hungary during the season. He wrote on 30 May 1790 that he 'cannot go to Vienna even for 24 hours; it's scarcely credible, and yet the refusal is always couched in such polite terms, so polite in fact that I just don't have the heart to insist on receiving the permission. Oh well! As God pleases! This time will also pass away, and the day come when I shall have the inexpressible pleasure of sitting beside Your Grace at the pianoforte, hearing Mozart's masterpieces. ...'

This brings us to the second of Haydn's reasons for wanting to be in Vienna.

HAYDN AND MOZART

It is not known when Haydn and Mozart first met, but they were certainly in regular contact by the beginning of 1785. In January of that year, Mozart attended what was to have been Haydn's initiation at the masonic lodge *Zur wahren Eintracht*, though in the event the ceremony did not take place until a fortnight later.

(Unlike Mozart, Haydn took little further part in masonic activities thereafter, although a number of his acquaintances were freemasons, including Hofrat von Greiner, who supplied the texts for many of his songs, and Prince Nicolaus himself.) We also know from a letter of Mozart's father Leopold that in January Mozart played to 'his dear friend Haydn' and other intimate members of his circle the six string quartets that he would later dedicate to the older composer.

The following month Leopold was himself in Vienna visiting his son and daughter-in-law. The evening after his arrival, there was a quartet party at the Mozarts' opulent flat in the Domgasse, at which Haydn was present and heard again the last three quartets of which he was to be the dedicatee (K.485, 464 and 465). Afterwards, he famously remarked to Leopold: 'Before God and as an honest man, I tell you that your son is the greatest composer known to me either in person or by name. He has taste and, what is more, the most profound knowledge of composition.' It was a tribute repaid by Mozart himself in the unconventionally heartfelt dedicatory letter to the score of his 'Haydn' quartets as published by Artaria in 1785:

> *A father who had resolved to send his children out into the great world took it to be his duty to confide them to the protection and guidance of a very celebrated Man, especially when the latter by good fortune was at the same time his best Friend.*
>
> *Here they are then, O great Man and my dearest Friend, these six children of mine. . . . From this moment I resign to you all my rights in them. . . .*

It is perhaps not surprising that the two greatest living composers should recognize each other and be influenced by each other's music. It is more remarkable that they should have admired each other so freely and so publicly. Mozart, never a man given to self-deprecation, is reputed to have said to the Bohemian composer Koželuch: 'even if you and I were melted together, the result would be a far cry from Haydn'. That Haydn, already the most celebrated composer in Europe, should have gone out of his way to evangelize for Mozart's greater talent is another heartwarming testimony to his generosity of spirit. Hearing of Mozart's untimely death in 1791, he told Dr. Burney: 'I have often been flattered by my friends as having some genius, but he was much my superior'; and he wrote from London to Marianne von Genzinger: 'Posterity will not see such a talent again in 100 years!' It is notable that once he had come into contact with Mozart's music, he steered away from those forms in which the younger composer's genius showed itself most characteristically, especially opera and the piano concerto. 'Where Mozart is,' he once said, 'Haydn cannot show himself.' No music since that of C.P.E. Bach had affected him so profoundly.

Most surprising of all is the fact that the two men became close friends – 'like brothers' according to their mutual friend the Abbé Stadler. Mozart was twenty-nine, supremely self-confident, disciplined only in his musical life, and a precociously early developer. Haydn was fifty-three, modest and phlegmatic, orderly and businesslike in all his affairs, and so slow to develop that had he died at the same age as Mozart we should hardly remember him today. Mozart's facility in composition is legendary, if often overstated; Haydn confessed that he always found writing hard work and would often break off to tell his rosary in the hope that new ideas would come to him.

Despite such differences of age, temperament and musical personality, however, they clearly held each other in deep personal regard. Haydn was one of only two friends Mozart invited to the first rehearsals of his opera *Così fan tutte*, and Mozart was included in the select circle who saw Haydn off on his first journey to London at the end of 1790. We know little about Haydn's visits to Vienna in the second half of the 1780s except that they were less frequent than he would have liked, but it seems reasonable to assume that the two men met whenever they could.

Perhaps the most moving document of this extraordinary friendship is the 1787 letter to Roth in Prague, part of which has already been quoted. After his encomium to Mozart as an operatic composer, Haydn goes on to say:

> *If only I could impress on the soul of every friend of music, and on high personages in particular, how inimitable are Mozart's works, how profound, how musically intelligent, how extraordinarily sensitive! (for this is how I understand them, how I feel them) – why then the nations would vie with each other to possess such a jewel within their frontiers. . . . It enrages me to*

think that this incomparable Mozart is not yet engaged by some imperial or royal court! Forgive me if I lose my head: but I love the man so dearly.

Mozart's *Le nozze di Figaro* was one of the operas Haydn was preparing for performance at Eszterháza in the late summer of 1790 when Prince Nicolaus, now seventy-six years old and already weakened by depression at the death of his wife earlier in the year, suspended all performances to consult his doctor in Vienna. The Eszterháza opera season was never to resume. On 28 September the prince died, leaving Haydn a pension of 1,000 gulden a year in his will. His son and heir, Prince Anton, had no love for Eszterháza; nor did he share his father's 'insatiable appetite for music', which in recent years had become so great a constraint on Haydn's freedom. Within two days of his succession, he dismissed the entire orchestra, breaking up the musical establishment which had been his father's pride and the focus of Haydn's life for thirty years.

Haydn himself remained *Kapellmeister* in name and salary, but with no prescribed duties. He was scarcely slower to act than his new employer. There was nothing now to keep him at Eszterháza and much to draw him away. He moved immediately to Vienna.

CHAPTER 7
THE ENGLISH TRIUMPHS
(1790–95)

♦ *London visits*
♦ *Haydn and Beethoven*

aydn took rooms with a friend, intending to make the most of life in the capital, but events continued to move at a dizzying speed. Almost immediately, offers began to arrive from admirers who had heard of his changed circumstances and sought to lure him to their courts. These included Prince Grassalkovich, who offered him the post of *Kapellmeister* in Pressburg (now Bratislava), and King Ferdinand IV of Naples, for whom he had written the works for *lire organizzate*. Haydn's unstinting loyalty to Prince Nicolaus had prevented him from accepting any of the increasingly tempting invitations that had come his way in recent years. Now suddenly he was spoilt for choice.

Someone else who heard of Prince Nicolaus' death was the London-based impresario Johann Peter Salomon, who was in Cologne en route to Italy to sign up soloists for his next concert season. He boarded the first coach to Vienna and marched straight into Haydn's rooms with the memorable announcement: 'I am Salomon from London and have come to fetch you. Tomorrow we shall conclude an agreement.' Haydn was clearly very impressed with both his determination and his terms (£1,200 for a new opera, six symphonies, compositions for twenty concert appearances and an advance against receipts from a benefit concert) and, with Prince Anton's gracious permission, an agreement was reached by 8 December. Haydn was standing at the threshold of his greatest triumphs and of what he would often say were the happiest years of his life.

THE FIRST LONDON VISIT

Throughout the 1780s the English musical press had been buzzing with rumours that Haydn was about to visit London. His music had long been idolized in the capital, one newspaper even going so far as to suggest that 'this wonderful man' should be kidnapped from the 'dungeon' of his servitude to a 'miserable German Prince' for the glory of 'Great Britain, the country for which his music seems to be made'. It was not for nothing that Salomon would have engraved on his tombstone at Westminster Abbey the words 'He brought Haydn to England'.

On 15 December 1790, just a week after signing their contract, Haydn and Salomon left for London together. According to Dies, Mozart had tried to dissuade his friend, arguing 'you have had no training for the great world, and you speak too few languages'. 'Oh!' replied Haydn, 'my language is understood all over the world!' When Haydn came to leave, Dies says, Mozart told him with tears in his eyes that this was probably the last time the two men would see each other alive – a not unreasonable assumption perhaps, given Haydn's relatively advanced age and the rigours of eighteenth-century travel. In fact, by the time Haydn returned to Vienna in 1792, Mozart himself was dead. He was thirty-five.

Haydn arrived in London on 2 January 1791, having weathered a rough Channel crossing, his first sight of the sea he had pictured in music in *Der krumme Teufel* and *La vera costanza*. Owing to the efficiency of Salomon's advance marketing, he immediately found himself plunged into a whirlpool of social activity, writing to Marianne von Genzinger in weary wonderment at the end of his first week: 'My arrival caused a great sensation throughout the whole city, and I went the round of all the newspapers for 3 successive days. Everyone wants to know me. I had to dine out 6 times up to now, and if I wanted, I could dine out every day.' Burney published a verse panegyric to the 'great master', and his public appearances were greeted with such applause as 'had not been conferred on anyone for 50 years'. He was shown special favour by the Prince of Wales (the future George IV) at a court ball for the queen's birthday and took part in musical evenings with him and other members of the royal family. As can be seen from the eclectic notebooks he kept during his London visits, he was soon acquainted with a wide cross-section of the music-loving

aristocracy and middle classes and was clearly judged an enter-
taining guest as well as one to be seen with. This homage
occasionally took weird forms. People would sometimes simply
walk up to Haydn, examine him from head to foot, and say 'You
are a great man'; and at one party given in his honour he noticed
that the hostesses were all wearing his name embroidered on their
headdresses in gold thread. He was a particular success with
women, finding a romantic admirer in Rebecca Schroeter, the
young widow of a former Master of the King's Musick, whose
affectionate letters he copied into his notebooks and whose
advances he evidently reciprocated.

If all this lionizing was somewhat overwhelming for a man
who had only weeks before emerged from the cocoon of princely
service, Haydn seems also to have relished the experience. It is
a tribute to his self-sufficiency, though, that he remained wholly
unspoilt by it, finding it rather a distraction, albeit a pleasant one,
from the important business of composing. This he pursued in a
room situated across the road from his elegant lodgings in Great
Pulteney Street.

The musical life of the huge and sometimes daunting me-
tropolis was rich and varied, with at least one musical event a
night during the season. It was dominated by the rivalry between
two concert series: the Professional Concerts on the one hand and
Salomon's more recently established series at the Hanover
Square Rooms on the other. Haydn was of course the star attraction of the Salomon concerts, which began on 11 March with a
spectacularly successful performance of his *Symphony No.92* ('*Oxford*') directed by the composer from the piano. Burney, who was
present, recorded that Haydn's presence 'so electrified the audience, as to excite an attention and a pleasure superior to any that
had ever, to my knowledge, been caused by instrumental music
in England.'

The *Morning Chronicle*'s reviewer called Haydn 'the first
musical genius of the age' and expressed the hope – to be
repeated in many quarters during his two London visits – that he
could be persuaded to stay in England permanently. The remaining eleven concerts were equally successful, with Haydn directing his *Symphonies Nos.90 & 92*, as well as the specially written
Nos.95 (his last symphony in a minor key) & 96 (probably the
first to be performed, though not the first numerically, of the

so-called '*London*' *Symphonies*). He also presented the quartets Op.64 and the cantata *Arianna a Naxos*.

Haydn's operatic career in London proved less auspicious. His final opera, *L'anima del filosofo*, specially written for the opera company of John Gallini and later published in part as *Orfeo ed Eurydice*, was to have been performed at the Pantheon, but it fell foul of intrigues designed to safeguard the supremacy of the rival King's Theatre and never appeared on the London stage.

In May, Haydn had a hugely profitable benefit concert. More significant for his future musical development, however, was the Handel Festival that took place during the same month. Haydn was deeply affected by hearing Handel's great oratorios performed in Westminster Abbey by gigantic forces – over a thousand strong according to some reports – and exclaimed during the *Messiah* 'He is the father of us all'. It speaks volumes for the openness to new musical experiences of this man of almost sixty that 'he confessed to [his biographer Carpani] that when he heard Handel's music in London, he was so struck by it that he began his studies all over again as if he had known nothing until that time.' That reevaluation was to leave its most enduring mark in Haydn's own great oratorios, *The Creation* and *The Seasons*.

Shortly after the concert season ended in June, Haydn received another gratifying token of the esteem in which he was held in England when the University of Oxford conferred on him the honorary degree of Doctor of Music. He attended the solemn ceremony at the Sheldonian Theatre in Oxford and delighted the audience by raising the ends of his gown and saying loudly in English 'I thank you'. Among the works performed at the concert in the evening was Haydn's *Symphony No.92*, hence the nickname ('*Oxford*') by which it is still known.

The composer himself set great store by this recognition of his talents by one of the world's greatest academic institutions, and often signed himself Doctor of Music. It must have seemed a formal vindication of his oft-stated principle that in the final analysis academic correctness came second to aesthetic effect: 'If I thought something was beautiful,' he told Dies, 'and it seemed to me likely to satisfy the ear and the heart, and I should have had to sacrifice such beauty to dried-up pedantry, then I preferred to let a little grammatical blunder stand.'

At about the same time he signed a new contract with

Salomon for the 1792 season, which he kept despite a respectful but unambiguous letter from Prince Anton commanding him to return to Eszterháza, where his absence was proving inconvenient. (Haydn assumed he would be dismissed as a result, but the prince seems to have taken his refusal in good part.) In the summer months he stayed with friends in the country, did some sightseeing and tried to brush up his virtually non-existent English. Even during what was effectively the first holiday of his life, however, he continued to compose, working on *Symphonies Nos.93, 94 (Surprise)* and *98* for the 1792 season. Indeed, he wrote to Marianne in January 1792: 'I never in my life wrote so much in one year as I have here during this past one, but now I am completely exhausted.'

Nonetheless, towards the end of 1791 he found time to attend the Lord Mayor's banquet, where he deplored the quality of the music and the boorish drinking of the other diners, and was a guest of the Duke of York, whose charming young Duchess could hum his symphonies from memory.

The 1792 season was marked by a potentially ugly heightening of the competition between Salomon's series and the Professional Concerts when the latter engaged Haydn's own pupil Ignaz Pleyel as a rival attraction. They also lost no opportunity to cast doubt on the older composer's ability to produce new and worthwhile music. Typically, Haydn not only disproved the latter contention, but also refused to allow professional rivalry to undermine a friendship: 'Pleyel's presumption is sharply criticized,' he wrote to Marianne, 'but I love him just the same. I always go to his concerts and am the first to applaud him.'

The season opened with another sensation: the first performance of *Symphony No.93*, two movements of which had to be encored. Subsequent concerts premiered the *Symphony No.98*, the intense slow movement of which begins with a theme derived from '*God save the King*' and has been seen by some as an elegy to Mozart, whose death in December 1791 had affected Haydn profoundly; the sunny *Sinfonia concertante* for violin, cello, oboe bassoon and orchestra, called simply *Concertante* by the composer and still one of his most popular works; and *Symphonies No.97*, which he seems to have saved for his hugely successful benefit concert in May, and *No.94*, the *Surprise*. With the possible exception of the *Emperor's Hymn* (now the German national anthem), this symphony is Haydn's best known single composition. The work derives its nickname from the slow movement, which states its deceptively simple theme, first *piano*, then *pianissimo*, before jolting the listener with a wholly unexpected *fortissimo* stroke from the full orchestra (though the story that Haydn intended it to wake any members of his audience who had dozed off is apocryphal). The dramatic madrigal *The Storm* was also premiered during the 1792 season.

In addition to the works written specifically for Salomon's concerts, Haydn's first London visit also saw the composition of his *Original Canzonettas* to poems by Anne Hunter (the wife of the surgeon John Hunter who, in one of the more bizarre episodes of the English trip, attempted to operate on Haydn by force to remove the nasal polyp from which he had suffered all his life!). He also began a mammoth cycle of Scottish folksong settings, initially for the struggling publisher William Napier; this was eventually to run to almost four-hundred songs, though many seem to have been the work of pupils.

Once the season was over Haydn put in a vigorous round of sightseeing before his departure for Vienna, attending the famous Vauxhall pleasure gardens, visiting Windsor and going to the races at Ascot. He was also a guest of that inveterate collector of famous men, James Boswell, and of the astronomer William Herschel, still feted for his discovery of Uranus a decade earlier, who gave him a demonstration of his celebrated telescope.

Haydn left London for Vienna in late June at the end of an eighteen-month stay that had given him his first real taste of liberty – 'how sweet this bit of freedom really is!' he wrote to Marianne – and had by any standards been a triumph. In the process he had earned the equivalent of twelve times his Ester-házy salary.

On the way home he stopped first in Bonn and then in Frankfurt. At the latter he mended his fences with Prince Anton, who was there for the coronation of Leopold II as Holy Roman Emperor. At the former he met the gifted twenty-two-year-old violist of the court orchestra, who presented him with a cantata he had written a couple of years earlier and arranged to come and study with Haydn in Vienna as soon as he could get his employer's permission to do so. The young man's name was Ludwig van Beethoven.

HAYDN AND BEETHOVEN

Haydn's return to Vienna in July 1792 seems to have gone largely unremarked outside his personal circle, itself tragically depleted by the early death of Mozart and soon to be rocked by that of Haydn's closest friend, Marianne von Genzinger, in January 1793. Certainly, there were none of the fanfares that greeted his arrival in England the previous year, though after the frenetic pace of his London life the sexagenarian composer may well have found it something of a relief no longer to be the centre of attention.

In August 1793 he bought the house in the Viennese suburb of Gumpendorf that was to be his home for the rest of his life and which is today a Haydn museum. In the same year Count Harrach raised in the grounds of his castle at Rohrau a monument to the son of his family's former cook. (The statue, a plastercast of which Haydn kept in his house until he died, can still be seen in the composer's birthplace.) From the point of view of musical history, however, Haydn's association with Beethoven is the most significant development of the otherwise relatively uneventful interlude between his return to Vienna and his second visit to England in January 1794.

Beethoven arrived in the imperial capital in November, hoping, as his patron Count Waldstein put it in a famous valedictory note, to 'receive Mozart's spirit from the hands of Haydn'. His studies, which began shortly afterwards, focused on strict counterpoint and were based on the *vade mecum* of Haydn's own formative years, Fux's *Gradus ad Parnassum*. Haydn was clearly deeply impressed by the young man's talent, writing to his employer, the Elector of Cologne, that 'Beethoven will in time fill the position of one of Europe's greatest composers, and I shall be proud to be able to speak of myself as his teacher.' He was also characteristically attentive to his pupil's material needs. He charged him only a nominal fee for lessons, lent him funds to keep him out of the hands of commercial moneylenders, and petitioned the Elector to provide him with additional living expenses (receiving a very dusty answer for his pains).

As Porpora had done for him in his own youth, Haydn also introduced his protégé to the cream of Viennese society, taking him to Eisenstadt and establishing the connection with the Esterházys that would bear fruit many years later in the commission for Beethoven's *Mass in C* (1807). He seems to have borne with Beethoven's legendary arrogance, already pronounced despite his relative inexperience, and referred to him good-humouredly as 'the great Mogul'.

Beethoven, on the other hand, was clearly unimpressed with Haydn as a teacher. He was later to say that he 'never learned anything' from him – which, whatever its truth as regards the older composer's tuition, is patently untrue as regards his music – and he may even have taken parallel lessons in secret from the operatic composer Johann Schenk. There was no dramatic rift of the kind that disfigured so many of Beethoven's later relationships – there appears to be no foundation for the famous story that Beethoven fell out with Haydn because the latter advised him not to publish one of his first three piano trios – but a friend recalled that 'Haydn seldom escaped without a poke in the ribs' in Beethoven's conversation. (The same friend also noted, however, that 'all [his teachers] agreed that Beethoven was so headstrong and stubborn that it required bitter experience to teach him everything he had rejected in his formal lessons.') Beethoven dedicated his Op.2 piano sonatas to Haydn, for whom they were performed at a concert of Prince Lichnowsky in the autumn of 1795, and the two men often appeared at musical events together over the next decade or so.

Beethoven's attitude to Haydn's music was one of profound but competitive respect, and his debt to it can be heard at every level in his own work. At his first major Viennese concert in 1800, all the music not written by Beethoven himself was by Haydn or Mozart, and at Haydn's last major public appearance, a performance of *The Creation* in 1808, Beethoven was among those who knelt in homage to him. By then, however, Beethoven's own music seems to have left Haydn more than a little bewildered. 'His first works pleased me quite a bit,' he is reported to have said, 'but I confess that I do not understand the latest ones. It seems to me that he always writes fantasias.' The verdict of one of music's greatest experimentalists on her greatest revolutionary, it is a strangely touching admission.

It had been Haydn's original intention to take Beethoven with him on his next visit to England, which was expected to take place in 1793. In the event, however, the outbreak of the Napoleonic Wars in Europe, together with Prince Anton's reluctance to part with Haydn again so soon after his last sabbatical, delayed the return visit for a year. In the summer of 1793, after persuading Prince Anton to give him leave, Haydn concluded another contract with Salomon and spent much of the rest of the year working on the symphonies and quartets he would present during the 1794 London season. On 19 January 1794, accompanied by his faithful copyist and godson Johann Elssler, he set out once more for Great Britain.

THE SECOND LONDON VISIT

The pair arrived in London on 4 February, the day after Salomon's concert series was due to have begun. This second visit is less documented than the first, partly perhaps because the demise of the Professional Concerts in 1793 denied journalists the spice of musical rivalry, but also because, with Marianne von Genzinger's death, there was no-one for Haydn to confide in by letter. That his music was received as rapturously as in 1791–92, however, is not in doubt. The attitude of the English press in 1794 can perhaps best be summed up in a quotation from the *Morning Chronicle* after the first performance of the *Symphony No.101* (*Clock*) in March: 'It was HAYDN: what can we, what need we say more?' The brevity is itself a form of honour. On his earlier visit he had had the benefit of novelty; now he was known as well as loved.

In outline Haydn's second stay followed the familiar pattern of the first. From February to May he was deeply involved in the concert life of the capital, directing his new symphonies and quartets to universal acclaim. He had brought with him from Vienna the completed *Symphony No.99*, his first to use clarinets, together with the quartets later published as Opp.71 and 74 (the 'Apponyi' quartets), but, enthusiastically as these were received, the great triumph of the 1794 season was the *Symphony No.100*. Nicknamed the *Military* from the martial 'Turkish' effects in the second movement (a reworking of a movement from one of his concertos for *lire organizzate*), it brought the house down at its first performance and was probably Haydn's single most popular work during his lifetime.

Once the season was over, the composer defied his advancing years with another intensive tour of southern England, visiting Winchester cathedral; Hampton Court, where the gardens reminded him of Eszterháza; Portsmouth and the Isle of Wight, where he evinced an unexpected interest in nautical matters; and the newly fashionable city of Bath, his descriptions of which are considerably more glowing than those of Jane Austen, who was to move there seven years later. At the latter he stayed with the ageing Italian castrato Venanzio Rauzzini, for whom Mozart had written his motet *Exsultate, jubilate* more than twenty years earlier, and whose summer residence, overlooking the expanding city, rejoiced in the appropriately suburban name of Woodbine Cottage. (In gratitude to his host, Haydn set as a four-part canon Rauzzini's mawkish epitaph to his dead dog!) Also on his summer itinerary were Bristol, where he admired the profusion of churches, and Waverley Abbey in Surrey, where, as a devout Catholic, he lamented the effects of the dissolution of the monasteries.

He also renewed old acquaintances – no doubt including Rebecca Schroeter, to whom he dedicated his *Piano Trios Nos.38, 39* (the famous *Gypsy Rondo*) and *40* (XV:24–26) – and made new ones. The latter included the legendary double-bass player Domenico Dragonetti and the pianist Therese Jansen, for whom he wrote his famous last three piano sonatas, Nos.60 (sometimes known as the *English*), 61 & 62 (XVI:50–52), and to whom he dedicated his great final trilogy of piano trios, Nos.43–45 (XV:27–29). He also sat for the artist George Dance, whose pencil-portrait is almost certainly the best of the many likenesses of Haydn that have come down to us.

Throughout Haydn's second stay in England, the country was at war with France and the government was in the grip of paranoia, instigating repressive legislation to intern domestic radicals suspected of links with the French revolutionary regime. In January 1795 the war touched London's musical life too. Unable to find soloists prepared to risk crossing the channel in the midst of hostilities, Salomon was forced to suspend his concert series, transferring his services – and Haydn – to the Opera Concerts at the King's Theatre, Haymarket, instead. It was thus at the latter's series of mammoth concerts (the band numbered some sixty performers under the leadership of the violinist and composer Giovan Battista Viotti, himself a refugee from France) that Haydn's last three '*London*' Symphonies, Nos. 102, 103 & 104, received their premieres.

The 1795 season began on 2 February with the first performance of *Symphony No.102*, sometimes known as the *Miracle* after the story that members of the audience were saved from injury by a falling chandelier because they were crowding close to the stage in their enthusiasm. (The incident used once to be attached, as the nickname sometimes still is, to *Symphony No.96*.) On 2 March, London concertgoers heard for the first time the ominous opening drum roll that has given the *Symphony No.103* its enduring sobriquet. Two months later Haydn's benefit concert was another huge (and hugely profitable) success, its centrepiece being the composer's final Symphony, No.104, often illogically distinguished from its siblings as the '*London*'. It is a fitting climax not just to the composer's English triumphs, but also to his entire career as a symphonist. Indeed, the last six '*London*' *Symphonies* stand among the finest works ever written in the genre.

The day before the first concert of the 1795 series Haydn had again been a guest of the Duke of York, newly returned from leading troops on the continent, and had been formally introduced to the king and queen. An eye-witness reported the following exchange between King George III and the composer:

> *His Majesty said (in English) 'Doctor Haydn, you have written a great deal.' To which Haydn modestly replied, 'Yes, Sire, a great deal more than is good.' To which the King neatly rejoined, 'Oh no, the world contradicts that.' After his introduction, Haydn by desire of the Queen, sat down to the pianoforte, and, surrounded by Her Majesty and her royal and accomplished daughters, sung, and accompanied himself admirably in several of his* Canzonets.

Two days later, Haydn was a guest of the Prince of Wales and directed his works from the keyboard, as he was to do many times at Carlton House during his stay. He also became a particular favourite of Queen Charlotte, who invited him to numerous royal functions and tried to persuade him to make his home in England permanently, even offering him an apartment at Windsor as an inducement to stay. Haydn declined, no doubt damaging his standing at court in the process. But by now he was determined to return to Vienna. His three years in England had brought him unprecedented celebrity and a gross income some twelve times his previous life savings, but they had also been exhausting for a man of sixty-three. Quite apart from the social pace of London life, Haydn estimated that he had written more than 3,000 pages of music in or for England since 1791.

Another reason for his decision may have been the changed circumstances at home. Just five days after Haydn's departure for London, Prince Anton had died. His son and successor, Prince Nicolaus II Esterházy, wrote to Haydn in England telling him that he wanted to put the musical establishment back together again, with Haydn at its head. Unappealing though the constraints of court life must have seemed after the liberty of London, they also represented security and, for a childless man in a welfareless society, a comfortable old age.

On 15 August 1795, Haydn left London for good.

CHAPTER 8
THE FINAL YEARS
(1796–1809)

- ♦ *The last great works*
- ♦ *'Gone is all my strength'*
- ♦ *Death*

The beginning of Haydn's last great phase of creativity saw him once more an active *Kapellmeister*, spending the summer at Eisenstadt and the winter in Vienna, as in the days before the construction of Eszterháza, now abandoned to its eerie fate as little more than a gigantic storeroom.

His last prince, Nicolaus II, was by all accounts the least sympathetic of the four Haydn served during his years with the Esterházy family. His interest in music was unleavened by the deep understanding his grandfather had shown for the art, nor did he share the latter's respect for his *Kapellmeister*, either as a composer or as an individual. Indeed, it was only after the intervention of his wife, the Princess Marie Hermenegild, with whom Haydn was on cordial terms, that he abandoned the demeaning practice, long discarded by his predecessors, of addressing the composer in the third person. Haydn, so recently the toast of the English royal family, was no longer the man to accept such treatment as a matter of course, and on at least one occasion when Prince Nicolaus interfered in a musical decision, incurred his wrath by replying, with an audacity unimaginable in his earlier years, 'Your Highness, that is *my* business'. Relations between the two men warmed somewhat over the years, but there remained a wrenching discrepancy of tone between Prince Nicolaus' curt letters of command and the encomia now regularly finding their way to Haydn from musical institutions throughout Europe.

THE LAST GREAT WORKS

The prince's main interest was in church music, and it is to what the composer called his 'moderate command' for an annual mass to celebrate his wife's name-day that we owe Haydn's six last great masses of 1796 to 1802: the *Missa Sancti Bernardi de Offida* (or *Heiligmesse*); the *Missa in tempore belli* (*Mass in Time of War*, also known as the *Paukenmesse* or *Kettledrum Mass* from the menacing timpani solo in the '*Agnus Dei*'); the *Missa in Angustiis* (more commonly known as the *Nelson Mass*, because it was performed in the presence of the great admiral and his mistress Emma Hamilton when they visited Eisenstadt in 1800 on their way back to England after Nelson's triumph at the Battle of the Nile); the *Theresienmesse*; the *Schöpfungsmesse* (*Creation Mass*, so called because the '*Gloria*' quotes Adam and Eve's duet '*The dew-dropping morn*' from Haydn's great oratorio); and the *Harmoniemesse* (*Wind Band Mass*). With the exception of the 1798 *Nelson Mass*, these were all first performed at the Bergkirche at Eisenstadt, where Haydn now lies buried. Controversial in Haydn's lifetime for their supposedly unecclesiastical style, they are now seen to represent, together with the two great oratorios *The Creation* and *The Seasons*, the summation of that lifelong commitment to choral writing which had begun with the faltering *Salve Reginas* of his choirboy days.

Another choral work of this period is Haydn's version for choir and orchestra of *The Seven Last Words*, written after he heard another composer's choral version of the work in Passau while returning from London. He donated it to the Tonkünstlersocietät, who had made up for their earlier lamentable disrespect by making Haydn an honorary life member in December 1797, and, as with many of his late works, he conducted it for them and for other charitable causes (including the welfare of those wounded in the war with France) in his last active years on the platform.

A further contribution to the well-being of a nation at war was the *Emperor's Hymn* ('*Gott erhalte Franz den Kaiser*'), which was conceived out of Haydn's deep-seated patriotism and directly inspired by his observation of the rousing effect of '*God save the King*' on audiences during his London visits. First sung in the theatres of Vienna on the Emperor Francis' birthday in February 1797, it became the Austrian (and is today the German) national anthem. It also served as the basis for the slow variation movement (and the nickname the *Emperor*) of the third of his six great string quartets Op.76, which were commissioned by Count Erdödy and performed at Eisenstadt in September 1797. Hearing them in London two years later, Dr. Burney wrote to Haydn that he had 'never received more pleasure from instrumental music', calling them works 'full of invention, fire, good taste, and new effects'. Together with the two quartets Op.77 and the now immensely popular *Trumpet Concerto* (1796), the Op.76 quartets represent the only major instrumental works of Haydn's last period.

The real centrepiece of the years following Haydn's return from London, however, is *Die Schöpfung / The Creation*. Not only had Haydn been deeply impressed by hearing Handel's great oratorios in London; Salomon had actually given him an English libretto on the Genesis story that seems to have been intended for Handel himself. On his return to Vienna, Haydn took the unpublished text to his friend and patron, the Viennese court librarian Baron Gottfried van Swieten – once a friend of Mozart and a prime mover in introducing the works of Bach and Handel to Austria – who set about producing a parallel German version. *The Creation* is thus the first work in musical history to be conceived and issued in two languages at once.

Swieten was also instrumental in raising aristocratic subscriptions to fund the performance of the work, which, contrary to eighteenth-century practice, had not been commissioned. Indeed, there is good reason to see it as a conscious bid for earthly immortality by a composer who knew he could not now have many years to live. Haydn began work on the oratorio towards the end of 1796, pouring into it all his religious devotion as well as his vast musical experience. As he was to tell Griesinger: 'Only when I had reached the half-way mark in my composition did I perceive that it was succeeding, and I was never so devout as during the time that I was working on *The Creation*. Every day I fell to my knees and prayed God to grant me the strength for a happy completion of the work.' The task was finished in 1798, just days before the first private performances at Prince Schwarzenberg's palace in Vienna on 29 and 30 April. Carpani, who was present, wrote of the occasion:

> *I never saw anything like it in my life. The flower of cultivated society, both national and foreign, was gathered there. The best*

possible orchestra; Haydn himself at their head; the most perfect
silence; and the most scrupulous attention; a favourable hall; the
greatest precision on the part of the performers; an atmosphere
of devotion and respect on the part of the entire assembly . . . the
audience experienced for two consecutive hours something they
had never experienced before.

Another eye-witness account described the electrifying effect of
the great C major sunburst 'And there was LIGHT' after the
unprecedentedly audacious 'Representation of Chaos' with which
the work begins. Interest in the oratorio was so intense that police
had to be posted in the Mehlmarkt outside the prince's palace to
control the crowds, and rival musical events were completely
eclipsed. At its first public performance the next year, both the
crowds and the takings exceeded those for any previous theatrical
event in Vienna, and the subscription list for its publication in
1800 was headed by the Empress, members of the imperial family,
the King and Queen of England, and the Prince of Wales. *The*
Creation was already set fair on its path to become the most
spectacular international success of its composer's career.

Meanwhile, the strain of the composition had taken its toll
on Haydn, who had been so overwrought at the first performance
that he feared he might succumb to a stroke. In June 1799, he
wrote to his new publishers Breitkopf & Härtel, whose middle-
man Griesinger was:

. . . the older I get, the more business I have to transact. I only
regret that on account of my growing age and (unfortunately) the
decrease of my mental powers, I am able to despatch but the
smallest part of it. Every day the world pays me compliments on
the fire of my recent works, but no one will believe the strain and
effort it costs me to produce them: there are some days in which
my enfeebled memory and the unstrung state of my nerves crush
me to the earth to such an extent that I fall prey to the worst sort
of depression, and thus am quite incapable of finding even a single
idea for many days thereafter. . . .

Nonetheless, he continued to work, writing more Scottish folk-
song settings, his last three masses and the two Op.77 string
quartets dedicated to Beethoven's patron Prince Lobkowitz, but

most of his creative effort was channelled into another major collaboration with Swieten, the oratorio *Die Jahreszeiten* (The Seasons). The libretto this time was fashioned, none too felici-tously, from one of the most popular English poems of the eighteenth century, James Thomson's discursive blank verse meditation of the same title, originally published between 1726 and 1744. Once again, the strain of composition proved immense. In September 1799 Haydn wrote to a friend that 'when this new work is completed I shall retire, because of the weakened state of my nerves' and in April 1800, a month after the death of his long-estranged wife, he suffered a serious collapse.

However, the oratorio was completed by the following spring, and on 24 April 1801 was given its first private performance, once again at the Schwarzenberg palace, to rapturous applause. On May 24 and 25 both it and *The Creation* were given at court, with the Empress herself singing the soprano solos, and four days later *The Seasons* received its first public performance in the Redoutensaal assembly rooms. In an ominous early sign of the reaction against Haydn's music that would set in so soon after his death, the occasion was surprisingly poorly attended.

Haydn himself seems to have had mixed feelings about his last oratorio. He claimed that Swieten forced him into some of the musical scene-painting, such as the croaking of frogs in 'Summer', and when Carpani tried to congratulate him after the premiere he cut him short with the words: 'It pleases me that my music has pleased the public, but I will not accept compliments on it from you. I am sure that you understand that this is not *The Creation*. I am aware of it, and you must be aware of it too. But this is the reason: there the characters were Angels; in the *Four Seasons* [sic] they are peasants.' However, Haydn himself was of peasant stock and proud of it, and *The Seasons* remains a pro-foundly sympathetic evocation of the joys and privations of Aus-trian rural life.

Haydn often said that *The Seasons* finally exhausted him. In the latter part of 1801 he made his will, with its numerous generous bequests to friends and family, and in August 1802, after completing his last full-scale work, the *Harmoniemesse*, he was released from his official duties as Esterházy *Kapellmeister*. His career with the family had come full circle. More than forty years before, he had been taken on as deputy to the ageing Gregor

Werner, while effectively running the musical establishment in place of his nominal superior. Now the same role of executive Vice-*Kapellmeister* fell to the young composer Johann Fuchs; and in 1804 the job of *Kapellmeister* passed to Mozart's former pupil Johann Nepomuk Hummel, Haydn's brother Michael having turned down an offer of the post to stay in Salzburg.

In December 1803 Haydn made his last public appearance as a conductor at a charitable performance of *The Seven Last Words* for the Hospice of St Marx. The same year he had begun work on his last string quartet (Op.103), but, despite intermittent attempts to complete it over the coming years, was forced to abandon it after two movements, commenting a little wistfully to Griesinger: 'It is my last child . . . but it still looks like me.' After more than half a century, his career as a composer was finally at an end.

'GONE IS ALL MY STRENGTH'

The story of Haydn's remaining six years of life is one of ever-increasing recognition and ever-declining powers. Learned societies and musical organizations – including such diverse bodies as the 'Felix Meritis' Society of Amsterdam, the Paris-based Société Académique des Enfants d'Appollon and Institut National des Sciences et des Arts, the Royal Music Academy of Sweden, and the Philharmonic Society of St Petersburg – competed with one another to accord him honours. He even received gifts from private individuals, such as the Leicestershire stocking manufacturer who sent him six pairs of stockings embroidered with excerpts from his works, and his house in Gumpendorf became a place of pilgrimage for numerous admirers (including Griesinger and Dies, who paid regular visits, drawing the composer out and noting their conversations with him). Of all these tokens of the respect in which he was held throughout the European musical world, it was the award of a medal by the Vienna City Magistracy in May 1803 that he valued the most, saying that it made him think of the proverb '*Vox populi, vox Dei*' ('the voice of the people is the voice of God'). The following year he was granted the freedom of the city that had first become his home more than sixty years before.

At the same time his physical and mental health continued to deteriorate. In 1802 he had even had to buy a new clavier, because the touch and tone of his old one had become too much for him. Having always replied assiduously to letters, he now answered some correspondents merely with a musical visiting card on which were printed lines from one of his part-songs:

> *Gone is all my strength,*
> *Old and weak am I.*

However, after a lifetime of composition it was impossible for him to switch off, and in moments of inactivity he was tormented by ideas he no longer had the capacity to develop. 'I would never have believed,' he told Griesinger on 3 September 1807, ' . . . that a man could collapse so completely as I feel I have now. My memory is gone, I sometimes still have good ideas at the clavier, but I could weep at my inability to repeat and write them down.' To Dies he lamented:

> *I must have something to do. – Usually musical ideas are pursuing me, to the point of torture, I cannot escape them, they stand like walls before me. If it's an allegro that pursues me, my pulse keeps beating faster, I can get no sleep. If it's an adagio, then I notice my pulse beating slower. My imagination plays on me as if I were a clavier . . . I am really just a living clavier. . . . For several days now an old song in E minor has been playing inside me, one that I have often played in my youth. . . . Wherever I go or stay, everywhere I hear it. . . . But curiously, when I am so deeply upset that nothing helps me to escape the torment, and my song* 'Gott erhalte Franz den Kaiser' *once occurs to me, then I feel easier; it helps.*

Another visitor to the Gumpendorf house reported the poignant scene that greeted him as Haydn, the world's most famous composer, tottered towards him on his swollen legs and said to him with triumphant countenance, 'You know, today I really played my prayer [the *Emperor's Hymn*] very well, really very well.' The final years were also clouded by the deaths in 1805 and 1806 of his beloved brothers Johann and Michael, and by the ever-present threat of the French army, which occupied Vienna in 1805 and again a few days before his death in 1809.

In March 1808 he received a name-day tribute from his

former colleagues in the Esterházy band, and wrote an affecting reply to his putative son Antonio Polzelli, now a violinist at Eisenstadt, asking him to 'tell them that my heart will never forget them, and that it is the greatest honour for me, through the grace of my ILLUSTRIOUS PRINCE, to be placed at the head, not only of great artists, but of NOBLE AND THANKFUL HUMAN BEINGS.'

The same month saw his final moment of triumph – a grand concert mounted to celebrate his seventy-sixth birthday. *The Creation* was given in Italian under the direction of Mozart's one-time rival, the court conductor Antonio Salieri, in the beautiful old hall of the university in Vienna. Trumpets and applause greeted Haydn as bearers carried him into the hall, and Princess Esterházy, sitting next to him, gave him her shawl when he shivered. It was a highly emotional occasion, and Haydn was too overcome to stay beyond the interval, during which the leading lights of Viennese society, including Beethoven, crowded round him to pay homage. As the old man was carried from the hall, he had his bearers stop and turn him to face the audience, whom he blessed with tears in his eyes.

On 10 May the following year, the French army began its bombardment of Vienna. The shock of the first explosions proved the beginning of the end for Haydn. He still played the *Emperor's Hymn* every day, but he became weaker and weaker, and on 26 May, with French sentries posted at the door to keep him from being disturbed, he took to his bed for the last time. He died on 31 May 1809, in the early hours of the morning.

He was buried quietly the following day at the parish church in Gumpendorf, from where his remains were later transferred to the Bergkirche in Eisenstadt. At the official memorial service in the Schottenkirche on 15 June, according to one eye-witness 'the whole art-loving world of Vienna' gathered to pay their last respects. Mozart's *Requiem* was performed in his honour, and in the midst of war the soldiers of France and Vienna took turns in guarding the catafalque.

JOSEPH HAYDN: COMPLETE LIST OF WORKS

Conventionally, different categories of Haydn's works are designated in different ways, but the most consistent form of identification is by the groups, and numbering within groups, adopted by the Haydn scholar Anthony van Hoboken. The following listing follows Hoboken's catalogues (made in 1957 and 1971), but where other systems are in common use (e.g., for the string quartets and piano sonatas) these have also been given.

For reasons of space, some of Haydn's less prominent categories of composition (e.g., his vast output of Scottish folk-song settings) have been summarized rather than listed in detail.

Not all the works catalogued by Hoboken are authenticated or extant. Nor should Hoboken's numbering be taken necessarily to reflect chronological order of composition. The precise dating of much of Haydn's vast output is so problematical that no attempt has been made to include even approximate dates of composition in this listing.

I. SYMPHONIES AND OVERTURES

Symphonies:

1 in D; 2 in C; 3 in G; 4 in D; 5 in A; 6 in D (Le matin); 7 in C (Le midi); 8 in G (Le soir); 9 in C; 10 in D; 11 in E flat; 12 in E; 13 in D; 14 in A; 15 in D; 16 in B flat; 17 in F; 18 in G; 19 in D; 20 in C; 21 in A; 22 in E flat (Philosopher); 23 in G; 24 in D; 25 in C; 26 in D minor (Lamentatione); 27 in G; 28 in A; 29 in E; 30 in C (Alleluja); 31 in D (Hornsignal); 32 in C; 33 in C; 34 in D minor; 35 in B flat; 36 in E flat; 37 in C; 38 in C (Echo); 39 in G minor; 40 in F; 41 in C; 42 in D; 43 in E flat (Mercury); 44 in E minor (Trauer); 45 in F sharp minor (Farewell); 46 in B; 47 in G; 48 in C (Maria Theresa); 49 in F minor (La passione); 50 in C; 51 in B flat; 52 in C minor; 53 in D (L'impériale ; Festino); 54 in G; 55 in E flat (Schoolmaster); 56 in C; 57 in D; 58 in F; 59 in A (Feuer); 60 in C (Il distratto); 61 in D; 62 in D; 63 in C (La Roxelane); 64 in A (Tempora mutantur); 65 in A; 66 in B flat; 67 in F; 68 in B flat; 69 in C (Laudon); 70 in D; 71 in B flat; *72 in D*; *73 in D* (*La chasse*); *74 in E flat*; *75 in D*; *76 in E flat*; *77 in B flat*; *78 in C minor*; *79 in F*; *80 in D minor*; *81 in G*; *82 in C* (*L'ours*) (Nos.82–87 known collectively as the 'Paris' symphonies); *83 in G minor/major* (*La poule*); *84 in E flat*; *85 in B flat* (*La reine*); *86 in D*; *87 in A*; *88 in G*; *89 in F* (Nos.88 & 89 known together as the 'Tost' symphonies); *90 in C*; *91 in E flat*; *92 in G* (*Oxford*); *93 in D*; *94 in G* (*Surprise*); *95 in C minor/major*; *96 in D* (sometimes still called the *Miracle*); *97 in C*; *98 in B flat*; *99 in E flat*; *100 in G* (*Military*); *101 in D* (*Clock*); *102 in B flat* (*Miracle*); *103 in E flat* (*Drum roll*); *104 in D* (*London*) (Nos.93–104 known collectively as the 'London' symphonies); *105 in B flat* (*Sinfonia concertante*); *106 in D* (overture to *Le pescatrici*); *107 in B flat* (Symphony 'A'); *108 in B flat* (Symphony 'B')

Overtures:
16 items

II. DIVERTIMENTI (WITHOUT KEYBOARD) IN FOUR PARTS AND OVER

1 in G; *2 in G*; *3 in G*; *4 in F*; *5 in F*; *6 in E flat*; *7 in C* (*Feld-Parthie*); *8 in D*; *9 in G*; *10 in D*; *11 in C* (*Der Geburtstag*); *12 in E flat*; *13 in D*; *14 in C* (*Feld-Parthie*); *15 in F* (*Feld-Parthie*); *16 in F* (*Feld-Parthie*); *17 in C*; *18 in D*; *19 in G*; *20 in F*; *21 in E flat*; *22 in D*; *23 in F*; *24 in E flat*; *25 in C*; *26 in F*; *27 in G*; *28 in F*; *29 in C*; *30 in G*; *31 in C*; *32 in C* (Nos.25–32 are the set of 8 *notturni* for *lire organizzate*); *33 in F*; *34 in C*; *35 in D*; *36 in G*; *37 in E*; *38 in A* (Nos.33–38 are also known as *Scherzandi*); *D18 in D*; *G1 in G*; *A1 in A*; plus 3 other unnumbered works in G, D and D; 39–47 are doubtful or spurious

III. STRING QUARTETS

These are generally known by Opus numbers, which have therefore been given first with the relevant Hob. numbers grouped after them. Op.3 Nos.1–6 (13–18) are now known to have been written by Hofstetter and have therefore been excluded.

The Hob. numbers do not always coincide with the order of composition or therefore with the consecutive numbering system sometimes used to designate the quartets.

Op.1 Nos.1–6: *1 in B flat*; *2 in E flat*; *3 in D*; *4 in G*; *5 in B flat* (properly Symphony A, I:107); *6 in C*

Op.2 Nos.1–6: *7 in A*; *8 in E*; *9 in F* (properly Divertimento

II:21); *10 in F*; *11 in D* (properly Divertimento II:22); *12 in B flat*

Op.9 Nos.1–6: *19 in C*; *20 in E flat*; *21 in G*; *22 in D minor*; *23 in B flat*; *24 in A*

Op.17 Nos.1–6: *25 in E*; *26 in F*; *27 in E flat*; *28 in C minor*; *29 in G*; *30 in D*

Op.20 Nos. 1–6 ('Sun' quartets): *31 in E flat*; *32 in C*; *33 in G minor*; *34 in D*; *35 in F minor*; *36 in A*

Op.33 Nos.1–6 ('Russian' quartets): *37 in B minor*; *38 in E flat* (*Joke*); *39 in C* (*Bird*); *40 in B flat*; *41 in G* (*How Do You Do?*); *42 in D*

Op.42: *43 in D minor*

Op.50 Nos.1–6 ('Prussian' quartets): *44 in B flat*; *45 in C*; *46 in E flat*; *47 in F sharp minor*; *48 in F*; *49 in D* (*Frog*)

Op.51 Nos.1–7: *50–56* (the string quartet version of *The Seven Last Words*)

Op.54 Nos.1–3: *58 in G* (*Razor*); *57 in C*; *59 in E*

Op.55 Nos.1–3: *60 in A*; *61 in F minor*; *62 in B flat*

Op.64 Nos.1–6: *65 in C*; *68 in B minor*; *67 in B flat*; *66 in G*; *63 in D* (*Lark*); *64 in E flat*

Op.71 Nos.1–3 ('Apponyi' quartets): *69 in B flat*; *70 in D*; *71 in E flat*

Op.74 Nos.1–3 ('Apponyi' quartets): *72 in C*; *73 in F*; *74 in G minor* (*Rider*)

Op.76 Nos.1–6 ('Erdödy' quartets): *75 in G*; *76 in D minor* (*Fifths*); *77 in C* (*Emperor*); *78 in B flat* (*Sunrise*); *79 in D*; *80 in E flat*

Op.77 Nos.1–2: *81 in G*; *82 in F*

Op.103: *83 in B flat / D minor* (unfinished)

IV. DIVERTIMENTI FOR THREE INSTRUMENTS
11 items

V. STRING TRIOS
21 items

VI. STRING DUOS
6 items

VII. CONCERTOS
(a) **Violin**: *1 in C*; *2 in D*; *3 in A*; *4 in G*

(b) **Violoncello:** *1 in C*; *2 in D*

(c) **Double-bass:** *1 in D* (lost)

(d) **Horn:** *1 in D* (lost); *2 in E flat* (lost); *3 in D*; *4 in D*

(e) **Trumpet:** *1 in E flat*

(f) **Flute:** *1 in D* (lost); *2 in D* (spurious)

(g) **Oboe:** *1 in C* (spurious)

(h) **Two lire organizzate:** *1 in C*; *2 in G*; *3 in G*; *4 in F*; *5 in F*

For keyboard concertos see XVIII. below.

VIII. MARCHES
8 items

IX. DANCES
1 Twelve minuets; **2** Six minuets; **3** Sixteen minuets; **4** Six *minuetti da ballo*; **5** Six minuets; **6** Twelve minuets; **7** Fourteen *minuetti ballabili*; **8** Twelve minuets for clavier or piano; **9** Six *Deutsche Tänze*; **11** Twelve minuets; **12** Twelve *Deutsche Tänze*; **16** Twenty-four minuets for orchestra; **23** Minuet and trio in G

X. DIVERTIMENTI WITH BARYTON
12 items

XI. BARYTON TRIOS
126 items

XII. BARYTON DUOS
19 items

XIII. BARYTON CONCERTOS
3 items (all lost)

XIV. DIVERTIMENTI WITH KEYBOARD
14 items

XV. PIANO TRIOS
The piano trios are sometimes known by the numbers given in the *Doblinger* edition; these are therefore included (in parentheses) after each item below.

1 in G minor (5); *2 in F major* (17); *3 in C* (probably by Pleyel); *4 in F* (probably by Pleyel); *5 in G* (18); *6 in F* (19); *7 in D* (20); *8 in B flat* (21); *9 in A* (22); *10 in E flat* (23); *11 in E flat* (24);

12 in E minor (25); *13 in C minor/major* (26); *14 in A flat* (27);
15 in G (flute trio) (29); *16 in D* (flute trio) (28); *17 in F* (flute
trio) (30); *18 in A* (32); *19 in G minor* (33); *20 in B flat* (34); *21 in
C* (35); *22 in E flat* (36); *23 in D minor/major* (37); *24 in D* (38);
25 in G (*Gypsy rondo*) (39); *26 in F sharp minor* (40); *27 in C* (43);
28 in E (44); *29 in E flat* (45); *30 in E flat* (42); *31 in E flat
minor/major* (41); *32 in G* (31); *33 in D* (lost) (8); *34 in E* (11);
35 in A (10); *36 in E flat* (12); *37 in F* (1); *38 in B flat* (13); *39 in F*
(4); *40 in F* (6); *41 in G* (7); *C1 in C* (2); *unnumbered in G* (3);
D1 in D (lost) (9); *F1 in F minor* (14); *unnumbered in D* (15);
unnumbered in C (16)

XVI. KEYBOARD SONATAS

The keyboard sonatas are often referred to by the numbering of
the *Vienna Urtext Edition*, which reflects their likely chronology and
which is given in brackets following the Hob. numbers listed
below.

1 in C (10); *2 in B flat* (11); *2a in D minor* (21); *2b in A* (22); *2c in
B* (23); *2d in B flat* (24); *2e in E minor* (25); *2g in C* (26); *2h in A*
(27); *3 in C* (14); *4 in D* (9); *5 in A* (8); *6 in G* (13); *7 in C* (2); *8
in G* (1); *9 in F* (3); *10 in C* (6); *11 in G* (5); *12 in A* (12); *13 in E*
(15); *14 in D* (16); *15 in C* (-); *16 in E flat* (-) (doubtful); *17 in B
flat* (-) (not by Haydn); *18 in B flat* (20); *19 in D* (30); *20 in C
minor* (33); *21 in C* (36); *22 in E* (37); *23 in F* (38); *24 in D* (39);
25 in E flat (40); *26 in A* (41); *27 in G* (42); *28 in E flat* (43); *29 in
F* (44); *30 in A* (45); *31 in E* (46); *32 in B minor* (47); *33 in D*
(34); *34 in E minor* (53); *35 in C* (48); *36 in C sharp minor* (49);
37 in D (50); *38 in E flat* (51); *39 in G* (52); *40 in G* (54); *41 in B
flat* (55); *42 in D* (56); *43 in A flat* (35); *44 in G minor* (32); *45 in
E flat* (29); *46 in A flat* (31); *47 in F* (57); *48 in C* (58); *49 in E flat*
(59); *50 in C* (60) (*English*); *51 in D* (61); *52 in E flat* (62); *G1 in
G* (4); *XVII:D1 in D* (7); *3 unnumbered in E flat, E flat and E minor/
major* (17–19); *XIV:5 in D* (28)

XVII. SOLO PIANO PIECES

1 *Capriccio* in G; **2** Twenty variations in G; **3** *Arietta con
12 variazioni* in E flat; **4** *Fantasia* in C; **5** Six variations in C;
6 *Andante con variazioni* in F minor; **7** Five variations in D;
8 Variations in D; **9** *Adagio* in F; **10** *Allegretto* in G; **11** *Andante
in C*; **12** *Andante con variazioni* in B flat; F1 in F

XVIIa. PIANO DUETS
2 items

XVIII. KEYBOARD CONCERTOS
1 in C; 2 in D; 3 in F; 4 in G; 5 in C; 6 in F; 7 in F; 8 in C; 9 in G;
10 in C; 11 in D; F2 in F
Nos.1, 2, 5, 6, 8 & 10 are organ concertos

XIX. PIECES FOR MUSICAL CLOCK
32 items, including original works and adaptations of works by
Haydn and others

XX. THE SEVEN LAST WORDS OF OUR SAVIOUR
ON THE CROSS
1 Instrumental versions:
    (a) original orchestral version
    (b) version for string quartet
    (c) piano reduction (approved by Haydn)
2 Vocal version

XXbis.
Stabat Mater

XXI. ORATORIOS
1 *Il ritorno di Tobia*; **2** *Die Schöpfung / The Creation*;
3 *Die Jahreszeiten* (*The Seasons*)

XXII. MASSES
1 *Missa brevis* in F; **2** *Missa 'Sunt bona mixta malis'* in D minor;
3 *Missa brevis 'Rorate caeli desuper'* in G; **4** *Missa in honorem
beatissimae Virginis Mariae* in E flat (*Great Organ Mass*); **5** *Missa
Cellensis in honorem beatissimae Virginis Mariae* in C (*Missa Sanctae
Caeciliae*); **6** *Missa Sancti Nicolai* in G; **7** *Missa brevis Sancti Joannis
de Deo* in B flat (*Little Organ Mass*); **8** *Missa Cellensis* in C
(*Mariazell Mass*); **9** *Missa in tempore belli* in C (*Paukenmesse*;
Kettledrum Mass); **10** *Missa Sancti Bernardi de Offida* in B flat
(*Heiligmesse*); **11** *Missa in angustiis* in D minor (*Nelson Mass*);
12 *Missa* in B flat (*Theresienmesse*); **13** *Missa* in B flat
(*Schöpfungsmesse*; *Creation Mass*); **14** *Missa* in B flat
(*Harmoniemesse*; *Wind Band Mass*)

XXIIa.
Requiem (spurious)

XXIIb.
Libera me

XXIII. SMALLER CHURCH WORKS
(a) Graduals, offertories and motets: 9 items, 5–8 doubtful
or by others
(b) Antiphons of the Blessed Virgin Mary: 1 *Salve Regina*
in E; 2 *Salve Regina* in G minor; 3 *Ave Regina caelorum* in A;
4–6 of doubtful authenticity
(c) Te Deum and other choral works: 1 *Te Deum* in C;
2 *Te Deum* in C; 3 *Alleluia* in G; 4 Four *Responsoria de Venerabili*;
5 Four Hymns *de Venerabili*; 6 Aria *de Venerabili, Lauda Sion
Salvatorem* (doubtful)
(d) 4 items

XXIV. CANTATAS, CHORUSES AND ARIAS WITH ORCHESTRA
(a) Cantatas and choruses:
1 *Vivan gl'illustri sposi* (lost); 2 *Destatevi, o miei fidi*; 3a *Al tuo
arrivo felice* (lost); 3b *Da qual gioia improvvisa*; 4 *Quall dubbio
ormai*; 5 *Dei clementi* (lost); 6 *Applausus*; 7 *Miseri noi, misera
patria*; 8 *The storm*; 9 Unfinished; 10 *Scena di Berenice*; 11 *Die
Erwählung eines Kapellmeisters* (doubtful)
(b) Arias with orchestra: 23 items

XXV. PARTSONGS
(a) Duets: 2 items
(b) Songs in three parts: 5 items
(c) Songs in four parts: 9 items

XXVI. SOLO SONGS AND CANTATAS WITH KEYBOARD
(a) Songs:
1–12 *12 Lieder für das Klavier – Erste Teil*; 13–24 *12 Lieder für
das Klavier – Zweiter Teil*; 25–30 *6 Original Canzonettas*;
31–36 *6 Original Canzonettas – second set*; 13 additional items
(b) Cantatas and choruses:
1 *Deutschlands Klage auf den Tod des grossen Friedrichs Borussens
König* (lost); 2 *Arianna a Naxos*; 3 *Dr. Harington's compliment*;
4 *Lines from the Battle of the Nile*

XXVII. CANONS
(a) Sacred canons: 1–10 *Die heiligen zehn Gebote* (*The Ten Commandments*)
(b) 47 items

XXVIII. OPERAS
Unnumbered: *La Marchesa Nespola* (or *Il Marchese*) and three lost works: *Il dottore*, *La vedova*, and *Il scanarello*; 1 *Acide*; 2 *La canterina*; 3 *Lo speziale*; 4 *Le pescatrici*; 5 *L'infedeltà delusa*; 6 *L'incontro improvviso*; 7 *Il mondo della luna*; 8 *La vera costanza*; 9 *L'isola disabitata*; 10 *La fedeltà premiata*; 11 *Orlando Paladino*; 12 *Armida*; 13 *L'anima del filosofo* (or *Orfeo ed Euridice*)

XXIX. MARIONETTE OPERAS AND SINGSPIELE
(a) Marionette operas:
1 *Philemon und Baucis*; 1a *Der Götterat, oder Jupiters Reise auf der Erde* (lost); 2 *Hexenschabbas* (lost); 3 *Didone abbandonata* (lost); 4 *Opéra comique vom abgebrannten Haus*; 5 *genovefens 4ter Teil* (lost)
(b) Singspiele:
1a *Der krumme Teufel*; 1b *Der neue krumme Teufel* (lost); 2 *Philemon und Baucis*; 3 *Die bestrafte Rachbegierde* (lost); A *Die Feuerbrunst*; F *Die reisende Ceres* (doubtful)

XXX. INCIDENTAL MUSIC
5 items

XXXI. ARRANGEMENTS
(a) Folk-song arrangements: 398 items
(b) Other arrangements: 17 items

XXXII. PASTICCIOS
All contain work by Haydn and other composers.
1 *La Circe, ossia L'isola incantata*; 2 *Der Freybrief*; 3 *Allessandro il grande*; 4 *Der Apfeldlieb*

JOSEPH HAYDN: RECOMMENDED RECORDINGS

There is a vast array of recordings of Haydn's phenomenal output, with some categories of composition – such as the symphonies, string quartets and oratorios – being much better represented than others.

For convenience, the following listings recommend complete or ongoing recording cycles where possible, together with a selection of notable individual recordings. Couplings have generally been specified only where they consist of works by Haydn not otherwise included in the listings. The recommendations attempt to strike an illuminating balance between period-instrument and modern-instrument recordings.

SYMPHONIES

The symphonies are better represented in the catalogue than any other category of Haydn's work, and there are numerous fine recordings to choose from. The classic complete set by Antal Dorati and the Philharmonia Hungarica is newly available from Decca (⊗ on 448 531-2) and is also being reissued in stages on the Double Decca label.

Notable period-instrument recordings include the cycle from Roy Goodman and the Hanover Band (Hyperion):

Symphonies 1–5 ⊗ Hyperion Dig. CDA 66524
Symphonies 6–8 ⊗ Hyperion Dig. CDA 66523
Symphonies 9–12 ⊗ Hyperion Dig. CDA 66529
Symphonies 13–16 ⊗ Hyperion Dig. CDA 66534
Symphonies 17–21 ⊗ Hyperion Dig. CDA 66530
Symphonies 22–25 ⊗ Hyperion Dig. CDA 66536
Symphonies 42–44 ⊗ Hyperion Dig. CDA 66530
Symphonies 45–47 ⊗ Hyperion Dig. CDA 66522
Symphonies 48–50 ⊗ Hyperion Dig. CDA 66531
Symphonies 70–72 ⊗ Hyperion Dig. CDA 66526
Symphonies 73–75 ⊗ Hyperion Dig. CDA 66520
Symphonies 76–78 ⊗ Hyperion Dig. CDA 66525
Symphonies 82–84 ⊗ Hyperion Dig. CDA 66527

Symphonies 85–87 ⊗ Hyperion Dig. CDA 66535
Symphonies 90–92 ⊗ Hyperion Dig. CDA 66521
Symphonies 93–95 ⊗ Hyperion Dig. CDA 66532
Symphonies 101–102 ⊗ Hyperion Dig. CDA 66528

Other notable period-instrument recordings include the ongoing cycles from Christopher Hogwood and the Academy of Ancient Music (Oiseau-Lyre) and from Bruno Weil and Tafelmusik (Sony). On modern instruments, Adam Fischer's series with the Austro-Hungarian Haydn Orchestra (Nimbus) is being recorded in the Haydnsaal at Eisenstadt.

CONCERTOS

Violin concertos Nos.3 in A (VIIa: 3), 4 in G (VIIa: 4) &
1 in C (VIIa: 1)

♦ Tetzlaff, Northern Sinfonia, Schiff
  ⊗ Virgin Classics VC7 59065 2
♦ Standage, The English Concert, Pinnock ⊗ Archiv 427 316-2

Cello concertos Nos.1 in C (VIIb: 1) & 2 in D (VIIb: 2)

♦ Mørk, Norwegian Chamber Orchestra, Brown
  ⊗ Virgin Classics VC5 45014 2
♦ Coin, Academy of Ancient Music, Hogwood
  ⊗ Oiseau-Lyre Dig. 414 615-2

Horn concertos Nos.1 in D (VIId: 3) & 2 in D (VIId: 4)

♦ Clevenger, Franz Liszt Chamber Orchestra
  ⊗ Teldec/Warner Dig. 9031 74790-2

Trumpet concerto in E flat (VIIe: 1)

♦ Marsalis, National Philharmonic Orchestra, Leppard
  ⊗ Sony SK 37 846

Oboe concerto in C (spurious) *(VIIg: 1)*

♦ Lencsés, Radio-Sinfonieorchester Stuttgart, Marriner
  ⊗ Capriccio 10 308

Concertos for two lire organizzate (VIIh: 1–5)

♦ Peasgood, Goodwin, Haydn Sinfonietta Wien, Huss
  ⊗ Koch Schwann 3-1379-2

Organ concertos in C XVIII: 1, 8 & 10
♦ Alain, Bournemouth Sinfonietta, Guschlbauer
  ⊗ Erato/Warner 4509-94581-2

Piano concertos in F (XVIII: 3) in G (XVIII: 4) & in D (XVIII: 11)
♦ Ax, Franz Liszt Chamber Orchestra ⊗ Sony SK 48 383
♦ Koopman, Amsterdam Musica Antiqua (also includes *Double concerto in F for harpsichord and violin; Concertini and divertimenti XIV: 3, 4, 7, 8, 9, 11, 12, 13, F2, C2*)
  ⊗ Philips Duo 446 542-2 (2)

DANCES
24 Menuetti (IX: 16)
♦ Capella Istropolitana, Guth ⊗ CPO 999 108-2

6 German dances (IX: 12); 6 Minuetti da ballo (IX: 4), etc.
♦ Vienna Bella Musica Ensemble, Dittrich
  ⊗ Harmonia Mundi HMA 190 1057

STRING QUARTETS
The ongoing Kodály Quartet cycle for Naxos is due to be completed in 1997 with Opp.17 & 50. It comprises:

Op.1 Nos.1–4 ⊗ Naxos Dig. 8.550398
Op.1 Nos.'0' & 6; Op.2 Nos.1 & 2 ⊗ Naxos Dig. 8.550399
Op.2 Nos.4 & 6; Op.42 ⊗ Naxos Dig. 8.550732
Op.9 Nos.1, 3 & 4 ⊗ Naxos Dig. 8.550786
Op.9 Nos.2, 5 & 6 ⊗ Naxos Dig. 8.550787
Op.20 Nos.1–3 ⊗ Naxos Dig. 8.550701
Op.20 Nos.4–6 ⊗ Naxos Dig. 8.550702
Op.33 Nos.1, 2 & 5 ⊗ Naxos Dig. 8.550788
Op.33 Nos.3, 4 & 6 ⊗ Naxos Dig. 8.550789
Op.51; Op.103 ⊗ Naxos Dig. 8.550346
Op.54 Nos.1–3 ⊗ Naxos Dig. 8.550395
Op.55 Nos.1–3 ⊗ Naxos Dig. 8.550397
Op.64 Nos.1–3 ⊗ Naxos Dig. 8.550673
Op.64 Nos.4–6 ⊗ Naxos Dig. 8.550674
Op.71 Nos.1–3 ⊗ Naxos Dig. 8.550394
Op.74 Nos.1–3 ⊗ Naxos Dig. 8.550396
Op.76 Nos.1–3 ⊗ Naxos Dig. 8.550314

Op.76 Nos.4–6 ⊗ Naxos Dig. 8.550315
Op.77 Nos.1 & 2 ⊗ Naxos Dig. 8.553146

There is no complete recording of Op.17 in the present catalogue. A complete recording of Op.50 is available in the Salomon Quartet cycle from Hyperion as:
Op.50 Nos.1–3 ⊗ Hyperion CDA66821
Op.50 Nos.4–6 ⊗ Hyperion CDA66822

The Quatuor Mosaïques, who use period instruments, have recorded the following quartets for Auvidis Astrée:
Op.20 Nos.1, 5 & 6 ⊗ Astrée E8784
Op.20 Nos.2–4 ⊗ Astrée E8786
Op.33 Nos.2, 3 & 5 ⊗ Astrée E8569
Op.77 Nos.1 & 2; Op.103 ⊗ Astrée E8799

PIANO TRIOS
The classic complete set is the Beaux Arts Trio cycle, available from Philips ⊗ 454 098-2 (9). Notable period-instrument recordings include that of *Trios XV: 24–26* by the London Fortepiano Trio (⊗ Hyperion CDA66297), and the Cohen, Höbarth and Coin cycle for Harmonia Mundi, which comprises:
Trios XV: 12–14 ⊗ Harmonia Mundi HMC90 1277
Trios XV: 15–17 (Cohen, Hünteler and Coin)
   ⊗ Harmonia Mundi HMC90 1521
Trios XV: 18–20 ⊗ Harmonia Mundi HMC90 1314
Trios XV: 21–23 ⊗ Harmonia Mundi HMC90 1400
Trios XV: 24–26 ⊗ Harmonia Mundi HMC90 1514
Trios XV: 27–29 ⊗ Harmonia Mundi HMC90 1572

OTHER CHAMBER MUSIC
Baryton trios XI: 5, 96, 97 & 113
♦   Geringas Baryton Trio ⊗ CPO 999 094-2

Notturni for lire organizzate (II: 25–32)
♦   Lencsés, Dohn, Slovak Chamber Orchestra, Warchal
   ⊗ CPO 999 121-2 (2)

6 Scherzandi (II: 33–38)
♦   Haydn Sinfonietta Wien, Huss
   ⊗ Koch Schwann 3-1443-2

PIANO SONATAS

The complete cycle by John McCabe is available as a 12-disc set (⊗ Decca 443 785-2).

Another notable ongoing cycle is that by Jenö Jandó for Naxos, currently available as follows:

Vol.1: Sonatas 59–62 (XVI: 49–52) ⊗ Naxos Dig: 8.550657
Vol.2: Sonatas 42–47 (XVI: 27–32) ⊗ Naxos Dig: 8.550844
Vol.3: Sonatas 53–58 (XVI: 34, 40–42, 48) ⊗ Naxos Dig: 8.550845
Vol.4: Sonatas 36–41 (XVI: 21–26) ⊗ Naxos Dig: 8.553127
Vol.5: Sonatas 48–52 (XVI: 35–39) ⊗ Naxos Dig: 8.553128

A recording of *Sonatas 58–62 (XVI: 48–52)* on fortepiano by Andreas Staier is available on ⊗ RCA Dig. RD 77160.

THE SEVEN LAST WORDS
Orchestral version:
♦ I Soloisti di Zagreb, Janigro ⊗ Vanguard 08.2034.71
String quartet version:
♦ Lindsay Quartet ⊗ ASV Dig. CDDCA 853
Choral version:
♦ Nielsen, Hintermeier, Rolfe-Johnson, Holl, Arnold Schoenberg Chor, Concentus musicus Wien, Harnoncourt
⊗ Teldec/Warner 2292-46458-2

ORATORIOS
The Creation (in English)
♦ Augér, Langridge, Thomas, CBSO Chorus, City of Birmingham Symphony Orchestra, Rattle
⊗ EMI CDS 7 54159 2 (2)
♦ Kirkby, George, Rolfe-Johnson, Choir of New College Oxford, Academy of Ancient Music, Hogwood
⊗ Oiseau-Lyre 430 397-2 (2)

Die Schöpfung (The Creation) (in German)
♦ Popp, Hollweg, Moll, Döse, Luxon, Brighton Festival Chorus, Royal Philharmonic Orchestra, Dorati
⊗ Decca 443-027-2 (2)

Die Jahreszeiten (The Seasons)
♦ Bonney, Rolfe-Johnson, Schmidt, Monteverdi Choir,

English Baroque Soloists, Gardiner
⊗ Archiv 431 818-2 (2)
♦ Laki, Wildhaber, Lika, Choir of the Flanders Opera,
La Petite Bande, Kuijken ⊗ Virgin Classics VCD7 91497-2 (2)

The Seasons (in English)
♦ Harper, Davies, Shirley-Quirk, BBC Choir and Symphony
Orchestra, Davis ⊗ Philips 434 169-2 (2)

MASSES

The complete masses are newly available from Decca on ⊗ 448
518-2 (7) with the Choir of St John's College Cambridge, the Choir
of King's College Cambridge and the Choir of Christ Church
Cathedral Oxford under George Guest, David Willcocks and
Simon Preston respectively. Notable individual recordings, including some from this cycle, include:

*Missa brevis: 'Rorate caeli desuper' (XXII: 3); Missa in
honorem BVM (Great Organ Mass) (XXII: 4); Missa Sancti
Nicolai (XXII: 6)*
♦ Nelson, Watkinson, Hill, Thomas, Minty, Covey-Crump,
Choir of Christ Church Cathedral Oxford, Academy of
Ancient Music, Preston ⊗ Oiseau-Lyre 421 478-2

Missa Cellensis (Missa Sanctae Caeciliae) (XXII: 5)
♦ Nelson, Cable, Hill, Thomas, Choir of Christ Church
Cathedral Oxford, Academy of Ancient Music, Preston
⊗ Oiseau-Lyre Dig. 417 125-2

*Missa Cellensis (Mariazell Mass) (XXII: 8); Missa brevis
Sancti Joannis de Deo (Little Organ Mass) (XXII: 7); Organ
Concerto in C (XVII: 1)*
♦ Smith, Watts, Tear, Luxon, Choir of St John's College
Cambridge, Academy of St Martin-in-the-Fields, Guest
⊗ Decca 430 160-2

Missa in tempore belli (Paukenmesse) (XXII: 9)
♦ Cantelo, Watts, Tear, McDaniel, Choir of St John's College
Cambridge, Academy of St Martin-in-the-Fields, Guest ⊗
Decca 430 157-2

Missa Sancti Bernardi de Offida (Heiligmesse) (XXII: 10);
Missa in angustiis (Nelson Mass) (XXII: 11); Missa brevis
Sancti Joannis de Deo (Little Organ Mass) (XXII: 7);
Theresienmesse (XXII: 12)

♦ Vaness, Soffel, Lewis, Salomaa; Marshall, Watkinson,
Lewis, Holl; Hendricks, Murray, Blochwitz, Hölle;
Rundfunkchor Leipzig, Staatskapelle Dresden, Marriner
⊗ EMI CZS5 68592 2 (2)

Theresienmesse (XXII: 12); Missa brevis Sancti Joannis
de Deo (Little Organ Mass) (XXII: 7)

♦ Watson, Stephen, Padmore, Varcoe, Collegium
Musicum 90, Hickox ⊗ Chandos CHAN 0592

Schöpfungsmesse (Creation Mass) (XXII: 13)

♦ Cantelo, Watts, Tear, Forbes Robinson, Choir of St John's
College Cambridge, Academy of St Martin-in-the-Fields,
Guest ⊗ Decca 430 161-2

♦ Hendricks, Murray, Blochwitz, Hölle, Rundfunkchor
Leipzig, Staatskapelle Dresden, Marriner
⊗ EMI CMS5 65839-2

Harmoniemesse (Wind Band Mass) (XXII: 14)

♦ Spoorenberg, Watts, Young, Rouleau, Choir of St John's
College Cambridge, Academy of St Martin-in-the-Fields,
Guest ⊗ Decca 430 162-2

OTHER CHURCH MUSIC

Missa 'Sunt bona mixta malis' (XXII: 2); Missa brevis
Sancti Joannis de Deo (Little Organ Mass) (XXII: 7); Ave
Regina (XXIIIb: 3); Offertorium: Non nobis, Domine
(XXIIIa: 1); Libera me (XXIIb); Four Responsoria de
Venerabili (XXIIIc: 4); Salve Regina (XXIIIb: 1)

♦ Vallin, Monoyios, Tölz Boys' Choir, L' Archibudelli,
Tafelmusik, Weil ⊗ Sony Dig. SK 53368

Stabat Mater

♦ Bonney, von Magnus, Lippert, Miles, Arnold Schoenberg
Chor, Concentus musicus Wien, Harnoncourt
⊗ Teldec/Warner 4509-95085-2

Te Deum (XXIIIc: 2)
- ◆ Vienna Boys' Choir, Viennensis Chor, Vienna Chamber Orchestra, Gillesberger
  - ⊗ BMG/RCA GD 86535

Applausus
- ◆ Musoleno, Dolberg, Johnson, Byrne, Courtis, Haydn Vocal Ensemble, Picardy Regional Orchestra, Fournillier
  - ⊗ Opus 111 OPS61-9207/8

OPERAS

There is only one representative recording cycle of Haydn's operas – that by Antal Dorati and the Lausanne Chamber Orchestra, focusing on the operas written for Eszterháza. The sets, some of which include selections of Haydn's insertion arias for other composers' operas, are as follows (an asterisk * indicates that the recording is available on import service):

L'infedeltà delusa ⊗ Philips 432 413-2 (2)
L'incontro improvviso ⊗ Philips 432 416-2 (3) *
Il mondo della luna ⊗ Philips 432 420-2 (3) *
La vera costanza ⊗ Philips 432 424-2 (2) *
L'isola disabitata ⊗ Philips 432 427-2 (2)
La fedeltà premiata ⊗ Philips 432 430-2 (3)
Orlando Paladino ⊗ Philips 432 434-2 (3) *
Armida ⊗ Philips 432 438-2 (2)

Other notable recordings of Haydn operas include:
L'infedeltà delusa
- ◆ Argenta, Lootens, Prégardien, Schäfer, Varcoe, La Petite Bande, Kuijken
  - ⊗ Deutsche Harmonia Mundi HM/BMG 05472 77316-2 (2)

L'anima del filosofo (or Orfeo ed Euridice)
- ◆ Donath, Swensen, Greenberg, Quasthoff, Chor des Bayerischen Rundfunks, Münchner Rundfunkorchester, Hager ⊗ Orfeo C262 932 H

SONGS
Original canzonettas, Books 1 & 2
- ◆ Griffett, Tracey ⊗ Teldec/Warner 4509-97503-2

Scottish folksong arrangements etc.
♦ Mackay, English Piano Trio
 ⊗ Meridian CDE84222

Arianna a Naxos; Scottish folksong arrangements; selected canzonettas, etc.
♦ Bott, Tan, Burg, Pleeth, Beznosink, Kelly
 ⊗ Meridian ECD 84080

Selected songs
♦ Augér, Olbertz
 ⊗ Berlin Classics 0090442 BC

SELECTED FURTHER READING

The classic study of Haydn's life and works is the five-volume *Chronicle and Works* by the leading Haydn scholar H.C. Robbins Landon. The five volumes are:

Haydn: The Early Years 1732–1765 (London, 1980)
Haydn at Eszterháza 1766–1790 (London, 1978)
Haydn in England 1791–1795 (London, 1976)
Haydn: The Years of 'The Creation' 1796–1800 (London, 1977)
Haydn: The Late Years 1801–1809 (London, 1977)

Other notable works on Haydn's life and music are:

Haydn: His Life and Music by H.C. Robbins Landon & David Wyn Jones (London, 1988)
Haydn: A Creative Life in Music by Karl Geiringer (in collaboration with Irene Geiringer) (3rd ed. London, 1982)
The New Grove Haydn by Jens Peter Larsen (work-list by Georg Feder) (London, 1982)
The Master Musicians: Haydn by Rosemary Hughes (London, 1974)
Haydn: Two Contemporary Portraits by Vernon Gotwals (a translation, with Introduction and Notes, of *Biographische Notizen über Joseph Haydn* by G.A. Griesinger and *Biographische Nachrichten von Joseph Haydn* by A.C. Dies) (Madison, Wis. 1968)

Haydn's correspondence has been collected as:

The Collected Correspondence and London Notebooks of Joseph Haydn,
   ed. H.C. Robbins Landon (London, 1959)

Notable works on Haydn's music include:

The Symphonies of Joseph Haydn by H.C. Robbins Landon
   (London, 1955)
The Great Haydn Quartets: Their Interpretation by Hans Keller
   (London, 1986)
Haydn: The Creation by Nicholas Temperley (Cambridge, 1991)

The following *BBC Music Guides* are also available:

Haydn Symphonies by H.C. Robbins Landon (London, 1966)
Haydn String Quartets by Rosemary Hughes (London, 1966)
Haydn Piano Sonatas by John McCabe (London, 1986)

Index

CLASSIC *f*M

MUSIC
A JOY FOR LIFE

EDWARD HEATH

Foreword by Yehudi Menuhin

Music is a record of a lifetime's passion for a subject with which former Prime Minister Sir Edward Heath has been involved since he was nine years old. In this book – first published in 1976 and now updated in his eighty-first year – Sir Edward recalls his musical experiences, from his days as a chorister in his parish church to his work as a conductor of international renown – a career that began in 1971 when he conducted the London Symphony Orchestra playing Elgar's 'Cockaigne' Overture at its gala concert in the Royal Festival Hall.

From his friendships with Herbert von Karajan and Leonard Bernstein to his great musical loves such as Beethoven and British music, from music at Downing Street to a series of five symphony concerts he conducted for his eightieth birthday celebrations, Sir Edward gives a fascinating personal insight into his wide-ranging experience. Written with great knowledge and characteristic enthusiasm, *Music – A Joy for Life* will appeal both to those who already have a serious interest in music and also to those who enjoy music and would like a greater understanding.

£16.99   ISBN: 1 86205 090 2

THE
CLASSIC *f*M
GUIDE TO
CLASSICAL MUSIC

JEREMY NICHOLAS
Consultant Editor: ROBIN RAY
Foreword by HUMPHREY BURTON

'*. . . a fascinating and accessible guide . . . it will provide
an informative and illuminating source of insight
for everybody from the beginner to the musicologist.*'

Sir Edward Heath

The Classic fM Guide to Classical Music opens with a masterly
history of classical music, illustrated with charts and lifelines, and
is followed by a comprehensive guide to more than 500 composers. There are major entries detailing the lives and works of the
world's most celebrated composers, as well as concise biographies
of more than 300 others.

This invaluable companion to classical music combines extensive factual detail with fascinating anecdotes, and an insight
into the historical and musical influences of the great composers.
It also contains reviews and recommendations of the best works,
and extensive cross-references to lesser-known composers.
Jeremy Nicholas's vibrant, informative and carefully researched
text is complemented by photographs and cartoons, and is designed for easy reference, with a comprehensive index.

£19.99   ISBN: 1 85793 760 0   **Hardback**
£9.99   ISBN: 1 86205 051 1   **Paperback**

CLASSIC *f*M
LIFELINES

With 4.8 million listeners every week, *Classic fM* is now the most listened-to national commercial radio station in the UK. With the *Classic fM Lifelines*, Pavilion Books and *Classic fM* have created an affordable series of elegantly designed short biographies that will put everyone's favourite composers into focus.

Written with enthusiasm and in a highly accessible style, the *Classic fM Lifelines* series will become the Everyman of musical biographies. Titles for the series have been chosen from *Classic fM*'s own listener surveys of the most popular composers.

£4.99 each book

CLASSIC *f*M LIFELINES

To purchase any of the books in the *Classic fM Lifelines* series
simply fill in the order form below and post or fax it,
together with your remittance, to the address below.

Please send the titles ticked below

J.S. Bach	☐	Gustav Mahler	☐
Ludwig van Beethoven	☐	Sergei Rachmaninov	☐
Johannes Brahms	☐	Franz Schubert	☐
Claude Debussy	☐	Dmitri Shostakovich	☐
Edward Elgar	☐	Pyotr Ilyich Tchaikovsky	☐
Joseph Haydn	☐	Ralph Vaughan Williams	☐

Number of titles @ £4.99 _____   Value: £_____
(carriage paid within UK)

I enclose a cheque (UK only) payable to Bookpoint ☐
OR
Please charge my credit card account ☐
I wish to pay by: Visa ☐ MasterCard ☐ Access ☐ American Express ☐

Card number ☐☐☐☐☐☐☐☐☐☐☐☐☐☐☐☐

Signature_____   Expiry Date_____
Name _____
Address_____
_____
_____   Postcode_____

Please send your order to: Marketing Department, Pavilion Books Ltd,
26 Upper Ground, London SE1 9PD, or fax for quick dispatch to:
Marketing Department, 0171-620 0042.